Special thanks to all the family and friends who supported us throughout this journey, especially for their editing and proofreading skills, and their offers of both criticism and praise.

ISBN 9781713810084

The Dark Side of Duty

Table of Contents

Chapter One   5

Chapter Two   27

Chapter Three   55

Chapter Four   67

Chapter Five   80

Chapter Six   107

Chapter Seven   116

Chapter Eight   129

Chapter Nine   157

Chapter Ten   170

To the Reader,

      It is my pleasure to introduce to you a man named Charles Bell, and to serve as the literary purveyor of his incredible life. I was fortunate enough to first make his acquaintance as a co-worker, and, as we got to know one another, he shared with me a few of the stories from his previous career as a police officer. Impressed by the harrowing nature which characterized his years of service, as well as his monumental bravery in the face of circumstances which might make a lesser individual cower in fear, I asked him one day if he had ever considered transforming the details of his life story into a more permanent form. I told him that I had been writing for my entire life, and that I would consider it an honor to help him. He accepted the offer, and the outcome of our endeavor can be found in the following pages.

      As for me, your narrator and Charles' interviewer, you really don't need to know very much about who I am. I will serve as a conduit between Charles' thoughts and actions, and as a necessary foil. What I mean by a foil is simply that I have lived a life which, in many respects, has been the very opposite of my newfound friend. He witnessed suffering, tragedy, and death on a scale which I could not even imagine if I wanted to, and would not have believed that anyone could deal with personally without going crazy, had I not gotten to know him. It has been quite the experience for me, listening to everything that Charles has been through as an officer and a citizen, and I will never forget the lessons about the hardships of life that he has taught me. I hope you all enjoy what he has to say.

                       Dominic

Chapter One

"Everybody makes mistakes"

It was early January of 2018, in Cincinnati, Ohio, when Charles Bell and I met for the first time to discuss the writing of his memoirs. I had called him about an hour beforehand to confirm the meeting, and we both arrived at the agreed-upon location at nearly the same time. We exited our cars in an adjacent parking lot, and began the short trip down the gleaming white cement sidewalk to the local restaurant we had chosen. The streets were busy with traffic, but we seemed to be the only pedestrians out and about. The air was crystalline and cool, with only a few visible wisps of white above us in the sky.

As we walked to our destination, my mind was in motion, with thoughts of both the future and the past. However, Charles and I's conversation revolved mostly around issues of the present. He and I were an odd pairing, to be sure, having no discernable relationship based on our appearances. Charles is a sturdy six foot two and over two hundred pounds, bald, with glasses and a short mustache, and I, about half a foot shorter, a twenty-five-year-old graduate student with dark brown hair, brown eyes and a full beard. I had a black messenger bag slung over my shoulder, and both of us were dressed in a light jacket and jeans, as it was unseasonably warm for a mid-winter day.

"Believe me," Charles said, "I would love nothing more than to quit my job right now and live off my pension, but I've still got a family to raise. I've still got a lot of bills to pay."

"How many kids do you have again?" I asked.

"I have six children, in total. From ages twelve to thirty. Had three kids with my first wife, no kids with my second wife, and my third wife brought in a daughter from a previous marriage, and then we had two kids together ourselves. And one grandson from my oldest daughter, and he's a joy in my life because he looks just like me. The thirty-year-old lives in Columbus, him and his wife."

"And your last two are how old?"

"My last two are twelve and fifteen, so they're still in middle school and high school right now," he said.

"Sounds like you've got your hands full."

"A little bit. But they're good boys, they stay out of trouble, and they study hard at school," Charles said.

"Good."

"In speaking of studying, are you sure you'll be able to have time for this and doing your schoolwork at the same time? I know you're going to be busy with all of that," he asked.

I shook my head.

"I'll be fine, don't even worry. I'll make it work," I replied.

"Alright man, I trust you."

We walked inside the restaurant, and since it was the mid-afternoon, just after the lunch rush, there were not many customers. The dining room was bordered by thick-paneled panoramic windows, which let in a wide swath of sunlight and reflected off every surface that was glossy or polished, as most of the tables and chairs were. We sat down in a booth in the far-right corner, and a waitress approached to ask for our drink orders. Charles wanted a soda, and I asked for water. There was not an unusual reason why we had decided to meet in a public setting for that first interview, at least not that I remember, although it was a place we were both familiar with, and that might have helped us ease our way into getting to know one another.

Following a minute or two of further small talk, and after the waitress came back with our drinks and took our food orders, I brought out a journal from my bag which I had marked with the working title of our project on the front, and produced our means of recording the interview as well. Earlier that day, I had made the decision to go out and buy a digital voice recorder for the purposes of the interview, and all of the ones to follow. It was not an incredibly expensive device, but it would surely do the job I wanted it to.

"So, are you ready?" I asked.

Charles took a drink of his soda.

"Yeah, let's do it, let's go."

I hit the 'start' button on the recorder.

"Alright, so the first question is an easy one. Where are you from, originally?"

He shifted in his chair to get comfortable, and so did I.

"Well, I guess you could say I'm from a lot of places. I was born in Los Angeles, California, because that's where both my parents went to college and where they both met. My father was a computer guy back in day, back when the modern-day computer and computer technology was still being developed, so as a family, we used to call ourselves the 'computer gypsies.' We would go where the computer jobs were, wherever my dad's work would take him, which could have been any random place sometimes."

"Sounds kind of exciting actually," I remarked.

"Eh I mean, yes and no. Since we moved around a lot, it was a lot of hard work, a lot of going-it-on-your-own as a kid for me, just me and my brother really. There weren't very many opportunities to make any long-lasting friendships."

The experience of my youth had been just the opposite.

"That must have been tough for you."

"Yeah, it was a bit difficult, but at the same time it wasn't too bad. I didn't have many permanent friends, with my brother being the exception, so we were obviously close. But I had a lot of life experiences for a young kid. And family ended up being the most important thing in my life. That was what my parents always stressed to me, the importance of family. Me, my brother, my mom and my dad. We were all we had."

"Well that's good, right? I mean I think it might be better to have your parents and siblings as your best friends growing up than, maybe, to have a lot of friends but then not have such a good relationship with your family? Your turned out pretty alright," I joked.

"I guess I did." He cracked a smile and tugged on the hairs of his mustache.

"Well, can you tell me about them, then?" I asked. "What were your parents like?"

I nudged the recorder a little closer to him, hoping that our conversation was getting picked up over the din of the music playing above our heads in the restaurant.

"So, like I said, I was born in 1966 in Los Angeles, and my parents were both well-educated people, my dad having degrees in Computer Science and Mathematics from Cal Poly, and my mom, she studied nursing and psychology at Santa Ana College. My dad was a very powerful figure, a man who demanded respect, and you gave him respect. He had been a naval officer during the Korean War, and afterwards decided to begin his career in computer science, kind of branching out from what he'd done in the Navy. He had worked as a communications expert and radio controller, so he basically continued to educate himself on technological systems and computers as they grew more advanced. He covered all of the United States and sometimes in Europe helping to install new computer mainframes for various businesses and government organizations. And when he *was* at home, he was always reading and trying to teach himself about the newest developments in computers, and so you know, my brother and I had to be really quiet and not disturb him, and so most of the time we would play outside instead of indoors. And, as long as I can remember, we always called him sir, never 'dad' or 'father,' always 'sir.' He was a very serious, reserved, and formal man. Had kind of your stereotypical, tough-love attitude toward parenting, but not to our detriment."

"He sounds like an excellent role model, that's what I'd say. I'm sure he expected only the best out of you and your brother," I offered.

"He did, he was a strict father, very disciplinarian. We never misbehaved around him because we didn't want to cross him!"

"I could definitely see that," I said. "So then, what about your mom, what was she like?"

I could almost see the rush of memories flowing into his mind as I asked the question.

"Well, my mother, she was the one who we could goof off with, that was for sure. My mother was a very loving woman, absolutely amazing to me and my brother. She basically took over and did everything that you know, traditionally a father does, taking us to Boy Scouts, take us to sporting events, throw the baseball with us, and she did her best to keep us out of trouble and keep us in line when dad was away. She was wonderful."

I couldn't help but smile.

"Seems like they did a great job of raising you guys."

"Yeah, I think my parents did a pretty good job, they did. They were working professionals, so we had to get ourselves to school and get ourselves home, and they both wouldn't be back home until late, but they made up for it. The moving around all the time was difficult. Whenever my dad decided that there was a better opportunity for him in another state, no one really argued, we basically just packed up and moved. That was it."

Once again, this wasn't something I could relate well to, as I had stayed in one city for the entirety of my childhood, with a mother who stayed at home to raise my brother and I, and lots of friends who lived close by.

"So, can you tell me about all the places you guys moved to and lived?" I asked.

"Yeah sure, of course. So, a lot of different states, a lot of different places. We left California when I was about seven, I think, and moved to a place called Osceola, Wisconsin, which is right on the border between Wisconsin and Minnesota, where both my parents had gotten jobs in St. Paul. Lived there for about four years. Then when I was eleven, it was off to Nebraska for about a year and half. We lived in a little town out in the middle of nowhere called Tekemah. Next was Washington state, for even less time than Nebraska, I think about a year probably. We lived in a city called Vancouver, which is just outside of Portland, but across the river on the Washington side."

"All that before high school, huh?"

Charles nodded.

"Just about. After Washington we went back to Wisconsin, same town as before, and I finished out my eighth-grade year there and started high school. And then starting in my sophomore year of high school, we moved to Richmond, Virginia."

"A bit of a bigger city than the others, right?" I asked.

"Oh yeah. And I loved my life in Virginia. I had a great time in school there, I had a beautiful girlfriend, and it was all great until the day we had to move away again, which was around age seventeen. At that point, for the first time in my life, I had to disagree with my dad, had to tell him no, and tell him I wanted to stay in Virginia. But of course, that didn't end up working out in my favor. No matter how much I yelled and cried about it, I really didn't have a choice. My mom kind of calmed me down about it, told me everything was going to be okay, and I eventually got over it, but it was pretty bad, I almost ran away as a kid, you know, I was torn up about it. Anyway, it was for my senior year of high school, that was when we moved here, it was 1984 when we came to Cincinnati. My brother and I adapted to our new surroundings, made friends as we went, and tried to look forward to the future and the great things ahead of us."

"I bet you were mad as hell about leaving Virginia," I added.

"Oh, believe it man, I was not happy."

Our food arrived then, on simple white plates, just an appetizer for each of us, and we started eating. The nature of that first meeting between him and I was, somehow, at the same time informal and uncomfortable, and I was sure that Charles felt this too. It was almost like a scheduled appointment, or a brainstorming session between two business colleagues who were thrust together to work on a project at a moment's notice. We had barely known each other for three weeks at that point, and the task ahead of us was uncertain. There was a lot of trust that had to be in place for our partnership to work, which only time and experience would be able to provide, and we weren't quite there as of that first meeting. All we knew at that point was that our shared goal would only become a reality if we really wanted it to.

After finishing our food, we discovered that we were both short on time, as we each had pressing engagements soon after. I had to leave to go to the library to get started on a paper for one of my classes, and Charles had to be home in time for when his kids came back from school. After paying the bill, we walked toward the back of the restaurant and discussed the details of our next meeting.

"Same time, next Thursday?" he asked.

"Yeah, I'll be free." I grabbed my keys out of my pocket as we headed toward the exit. "I should be free every Thursday right around this time, so I think that will be good."

"Works for me," Charles said.

"You want to meet somewhere else, like my place or yours?" I asked. "I think we should go somewhere our conversations will be a bit more private."

"Yeah, that's fine," he said. "Maybe we can do it at my house, I'll let you know if that'll work out or not with the wife. Be in touch, man."

We shook hands.

"See you next time."

A week later, we reconvened, this time around the dining room table at my apartment. We had indeed decided not to meet out in public anymore after that first session. One of the main reasons, which I discovered when I went back and listened to the recordings, was that there had been a cacophony of unexpected background noise, with the music in the restaurant, the sounds of cooking and grilling as the food for the restaurant's dinner rush was being prepared, and even the consistent reverberations of the traffic outside. Furthermore, since Charles hadn't been able to clear out his schedule enough to have me come over to his house, we mutually decided that my place would be our permanent meeting location from there on out.

  At the time, I was living in a large, gated apartment community about twenty minutes north of downtown. My unit was a two bedroom and bathroom loft apartment, with light brown carpeting and a vaulted ceiling, a balcony, a fireplace, and an old-fashioned-looking metal spiral staircase which headed up to the loft, where the half-bed and half-bath was located. It was my peaceful corner of paradise in our otherwise crowded, Midwestern city. I was on the third floor of a building that was already high up on a hill, which provided for me an almost boundless view of the surrounding landscapes, and there was also a woodland area behind us that had a nature and running trail. It was secluded, quiet, and it was easy for Charles to step outside on the balcony to take a smoke break if he felt the need. I wasn't a smoker myself, but I had been acquainted with cigarettes in my late teens and early twenties, and so I would sometimes join him out there on a whim.

  As I set up the recorder to begin our second session, I opened my notebook as well, and began to examine what we had planned to discuss during this interview. My priority in the early days of the project had been to take down as much background information about the man himself we possibly could, as I believed that our audience might benefit from having this knowledge ahead of time.

"So, you served in the military for how long, was it?" I began.

Charles drew a forceful breath, in and out of his mouth.

"It was fifteen years in total, fifteen long years. Some of the best years of my life, though, I would say. Learned a lot about the world, and learned a lot about life in general as an Army serviceman."

"And that prepared for you a career as a police officer as well, I take it?"

"To a certain extent, yes."

"Well, can you take me through some of it?" I asked. "We don't have to get it all down today if we don't have the time, but I do want to get at least a partial sense of the person you were before you joined the police force."

Charles nodded.

"For sure."

I flipped through a couple of the pages in my journal while my interviewee gathered his thoughts, I guess for the sake of appearing as though I was searching for something important in my notes.

"So, I guess you can start anywhere you want," I finally said after a few seconds, when it became clear that he was waiting for me to prompt us. "Recruitment, first day of basic training, wherever you think would be good to begin."

He had to think for another few moments.

"Okay, so we'll start back in high school then actually, I've got a story that I think you'll want to hear."

"Cool," I said. "Need a glass of water or something?" I motioned over to my kitchen.

"I'm good, thanks."

"No problem."

He took another deep breath.

"So, the military days. Well, it all started on a really nice day in high school, and, it was late in the day when I got pulled out of class, got called to the office, unaware of anything, and when I get to the office I see Sir, sitting there waiting for me. The secretary told me that he had signed me out for the day, and at first, I thought something was going on, I was asking my dad, 'Is there something wrong with mom, what is it?' And he just said 'No, we have to go on a little trip to run some errands,' and that made me even more confused."

I gave a chuckle. "Yeah, no kidding."

"Once we got out of school and got into the car, that was when it all became clear. He started talking to me about the military, and about how every good man should go into the service, which was short for 'We don't have the money to send you to college,' but also, he really did want me to follow in his footsteps, he was hoping that I would go into the Navy like he did. So, it was off to the recruiter's office we went."

Once more, I really couldn't relate in this instance, as my own parents really didn't care what I did with my life, just so long as I was happy. Charles seemed to have had a very different upbringing in this respect, and probably in many other respects. I wondered how much of that was generational.

"Hey, well, at least you got out of school for a bit," I said.

"Well yeah, but I wasn't happy about that either, I probably would have rather stayed, instead of being forced to go somewhere I didn't want to go. I was still sour at my dad around this age for making us leave

Richmond, so anything he wanted me to do at that point in my life was always kind of a battle. But anyway. So, we get to the recruiter's office, and we walk into the Navy office first, of course. But they were out to lunch, and somebody there told me to come back later, and I was already pissed off that my dad had yanked me out of school just to take me to the recruiter's office, so I was like, 'Yeah whatever,' and didn't really much care for what the Navy had to say. We walked down the hall a bit further and saw the Air Force office, and all of them were throwing pens up at the ceiling when I walked in the door, didn't look very excited to see me, so that was a no. Stopped by the Marine's office, and at first I didn't see anybody inside, but then out from another room walks this big, scary looking lady who looked eerily similar to one of my teachers at school who I didn't like, and so immediately I just said, 'Nope, sorry, not interested' and stepped back out into the hallway as quick as I could, just told my dad that nobody was in there. And then finally, at the end of the hall, out comes the army recruiter, and he came up to me right away, shook my hand, and took me into a room where he showed me a recruitment video of sorts, and halfway through, I'll never forget, we're at the part where they show all the vehicles, and he points up at the video and says, 'Look at those tanks, they're like four wheelers with guns!' And at that point I was sold, if I was going to be forced to choose a branch of the military, that was going to be the one, and so I said, 'Alright, sign me up!'"

    I laughed pretty hard at that one.

    "That's a great story. So it was the tanks that did it for you, huh?"

    "Yeah, well it was the tanks and the fact that I was doing the total opposite of what Sir wanted me to do. But, you know, sticks and stones. So then, after I graduated high school, shortly after that, I had to go downtown, swear in, get on a bus, and they took us over to good old Fort Knox, which we called 'VietKnox' at the time. And that was where I went through basic training, and after that I stayed to get some more advanced training to learn about how to operate the tanks."

"Can you tell me a little bit about basic training?" I asked. Of course, I had friends who were in the military and who had gone through basic, but I wanted to see if the regimen had been any different thirty years ago.

"I mean, it really wasn't too exciting to be honest, you're doing basic weapons and combat training, how to shoot straight, how to drill, you're doing PT in the sand at three in the morning, and moving little rocks from one area to another one at a time, you know, just normal, build-your-army-mentality type activities, learning how to follow orders."

So, not all that different.

"When I graduated from basic, I went back to Cincinnati, and that was when I married my first wife, all because I was about to go to Europe and we weren't going be together for a while. But let me tell you, in hindsight, that was a bad reason to get married to someone."

"Everybody makes mistakes," I said.

He chortled. "Yeah, you're telling me. So, I find out I'm going to be stationed in Germany, and me and a bunch of guys that I was at basic with, we flew out of New York, and we go through Frankfurt and then into this little tiny outpost in the middle of nowhere, can't even remember the name of it right now. The only thing I remember in terms of a first impression is that there was the guard tower, a big fence all around the base, and then a bar, like a hundred feet from the entrance. That was it. So we went down a long trail to the base, got to our bunks and dropped our bags off, and we had some free time for the rest of the day, so we decided to go drink at the bar that first night, got real acquainted with Hofbräu, which is a German beer, and after a long night of drinking we crashed in some kind of storage room that night behind the bar. Crazy night, the beer they had was like double the alcohol content of American beer, and I was eighteen or nineteen, so that was a hell of a time."

"I'm sure it was," I said.

"Then the following morning, a van came and picked us up, bleary-eyed and still drunk, and we rolled off down into Böblingen, to Panzer Kaserne, the ex-headquarters of Erwin Rommel, who had been a Nazi General during World War II. And it was just history everywhere man, I'm telling you. I was a big history guy at the time, I loved my history classes, and I still am, all I watch on television is the History Channel. It was really just amazing, there were all these big gray buildings with the German eagle above the doors. You went over to the main headquarters building where the 7th Panzer division had been, and you go in and there were pictures of Hitler inspecting the tanks and troops, the building itself, the barracks, which then became American barracks. It almost seemed like there were soldiers still walking around, just history in the air and on the walls, and at night you could almost hear them. So, I was at Panzer Kaserne, and I was in the field doing drills for a few months, and I pretty quickly rose up to promotion status and got my own tank. Had a great crew of guys from everywhere, a guy from Rhode Island, a couple guys from Boston and Worcester, Massachusetts, so we pretty much had the entire east coast mafia in my tank. And we spent almost three hundred days a year out in the field, out on maneuvers, battle runs, gunneries, and border patrols, drills day in and day out. And then we'd get ready to go home, but we wouldn't be home for very long, it seemed like we were back stateside and then as soon as we had gotten used to being home we were right back in Europe doing tank runs again. But it was nice being in Europe too, you know, it's not all that big, right, so on the weekends we would take trips, we would go to Spain, we skied in Austria and Switzerland, went to France, visited almost every place you could go in Germany, so I mean, it was great experience overall. It broke my heart to leave Germany, I just loved it there."

"Definitely." I was jealous of the span of his travels. I made a note to myself to look up the spelling of the locations in Germany he had told me about, because I wasn't quite familiar with the names.

"So how long were you stationed in Germany?" I asked

"Well, it was the beginning of December and I spent my 19th birthday there, so I was in Germany for five years until I was twenty-four. Brought my first wife over there and had my first child, my oldest son, he was born on the base on American soil, so he had dual citizenship until he was eighteen."

"That's cool!" I said. "What about some stories from your time on base, any that you can think of that you would want to share?"

"Plenty," Charles said. "I could go on for days."

"Well, go right ahead, I won't stop you," I said.

He paused.

"So, for one thing, there were a lot of places to explore in and around Panzer Kaserne. There were rooms down below underground and there were also several long tunnels connecting the buildings, and you could just picture the activity that was going on during World War II.

The back of the base was all cobblestone, and there was a set of stairs which led down to a brick wall which had been put up, and that was actually the entrance to more tunnels which led even further out from the base, and that was so they could run the tanks underground out of the base and railhead them for transport. During the Carter administration, they had sent some EOD experts in there to inspect the tunnels, and of course it was all rigged and booby-trapped, and unfortunately, a couple of the guys they sent inside accidentally blew themselves up inside the tunnels while they were trying to dispose of the traps and bombs, and so the tunnels were sealed out of respect for the dead."

"Understandable," I said.

"But here was the cool part, so one day, we were doing PT out in the woods, running a different route than usual, and somebody tripped over an air vent which was for one of the tunnels, which had been overgrown by grass but still had some of the opening visible. So naturally, we opened it up, and we grabbed a guy by the legs so he could hang down into the tunnel with a flashlight to see what was down there. All the guy saw was shadows of objects covered by tarps, and so you had to wonder, were they tanks, was it armaments, was it gold or treasure? Because the Nazi's stole a lot of things, they stole from everyone. So, all these years I have sat and wondered, 'has anybody gone back into those tunnels,' because of course they probably run for miles, but since they were closed off, who knows?"

"Yeah I was wondering that myself as you were telling me about it," I said. "That's a cool story, sounds like you guys had fun in Germany."

"We did. Unfortunately, there were bad times too though," he said. "I was never at war, but the fact is that we were stationed in Germany during the Cold War for a reason, so we could be right next to Russia in case something happened. Reagan was pushing hard to get the Berlin wall torn down and to unite Germany, which he did, and so there was less of a need for us out there once the wall fell."

"Oh okay, I get it now. So all those tank runs and drills were all just getting you ready in case war broke out. Makes sense." It was great learning these historical details from someone who had been there where he was, essentially on the front lines of the Cold War.

Charles continued.

"So, I didn't see combat, fortunately for me, but it's dangerous being in the military regardless, we still had casualties."

"How so?" I asked.

"Well, basically, you know, because tanks are just big, metal, killing machines, and accidents do happen. People got hurt over there all the time, because we would railhead our tanks too."

I was unfamiliar with the term.

"Can you explain what that means?"

"It's when you have tanks that you have to get up a ramp and onto a railcar, for transporting them to different places, instead of burning the fuel and putting miles on them, and also because it tends to freak people out when they see a bunch of tanks." Charles said matter-of-factly.

"Right," I said.

"But accidents happened. When you're rail-heading a tank, you've obviously got the tracks on the tank that are sticking out from the railroad tracks about two feet, so you have to kind of hit the edges of the railcar right in the middle, so it's very nerve-wracking. One day, we had a new private who was helping to direct the tank driver in, and instead of standing up on the rail dock where you were normally supposed to be, he was standing inside the railcar, and he had a 113 behind him, that's another type of tank. And so, when a driver is getting a tank up into the railcar, the top of the tank is suspended in the air briefly, and then when you're up the ramp to a sufficient degree, it slams down due to the weight and gravity, and when the tank slammed down, the driver panicked at the sound, might have thought it was cannon fire, and hit the accelerator, and the private got squeezed between two tanks, almost cut him in half. They kept the tank in the one spot and notified his wife who was on base, and they got to say goodbye to each other before they separated the tanks, because when they did that he basically bled out and died from the mortal injury, there wasn't much they could do."

"Wait, so was the driver inexperienced, like was he a new driver as well?" I asked.

Charles thought for a second. "I wouldn't say he was new, he just panicked, really, that's all there was to it. Driving those things took a lot of skill and a lot of guts. We had another private who died, as the tank was being rail-headed, and he was stowing away the antennas, but we were on a road that had power lines running across it, and he didn't see them, and one of the antennas he had a hand on hit the power line, and he got electrocuted."

"That's sad," I responded.

"It was, but training is training, there's always risk. But, alright, so after Germany, after the wall fell, I went home for good, and then it was on to Fort Stewart in Georgia, the land of swamps, rattlesnakes, scorpions, and gators. I did a lot during my time based out of Fort Stewart. First off, that was where I learned to be a combat life-saver instructor, which means that we replaced line medics so they could just stay at mass units, and so you would take a combat soldier, an infantryman, and you would teach him to do everything a line medic knows how to do, and so once you trained one infantry squad guy to be a combat medic, then he could teach everybody else in his squad the basics as well. After that, I participated in what was the first desert warfare training group on American soil. If there is fighting in a desert, the tanks roll, and so we spent six months in the Mojave Desert at NTC, a hundred plus degrees during the day in a big metal box, and at night it would still be in the seventies but you would feel like you were freezing because of the temperature swing. Every time we'd get some food delivered, the wind would kick up and we'd get our plates full of sand, you know, it was just crazy. Then I went back to Stewart, but this time we were out in the swamps again, and we'd do tank runs out there, just in a completely different environment."

"So then how long were you at Fort Stewart?" I asked.

"I was there for a year, got out after a year and went into the National Guard, my son was getting to be school aged and I'd have a couple more on the way around that time, so I needed to get out of the military and start looking for a job where I could be home and be with the kids."

"And so that's what led you to becoming a police officer?" I anticipated.

"Not quite yet, actually," he said.

"Really?"

"Nope. So here's the thing you probably don't know. Back then, and this was only about twenty-five years ago, so not even that long, but back then, there was still a stigma about military personnel getting civilian jobs.

There was an assumption that all you could do was follow orders, and that you couldn't think creatively, and that you were just a heartless killing machine..."

I was taken aback by what he just told me.

"Totally different from the attitude today, completely different. Wow, I can't believe that," I said.

"Much different," Charles said. "I was working two other jobs at the time while I was in the Guard just to support my family, I was a pizza delivery driver, I was a mechanic, I did all kinds of different things, because vets couldn't get hired for good paying jobs at the time."

"That's so weird to me," I said, "I can't believe people ever thought that way."

"It was a struggle, it really was, but I got through it, had to work hard to stay afloat, but we did it. And then one fateful day, I was told by a friend at the Hamilton County Sheriff's Department that they were doing a round of hiring for police officers, and so I went down and applied and got the job."

"So that's where you started out as a deputy, was at the Sheriff's Department?" I asked.

"Yep. I was at the Sheriff's department for six years while I was in also in the Guard still, but down to part-time. And in the Guard, I essentially changed roles, I went from being on the tanks as a gunner, loader, driver, and tank commander, to being in the S4 shop, which is logistics, so I was the battalion ammunitions NCO. You know how the schedule is one weekend a month, right?"

"Yeah."

"Well my schedule was one *week* a month, because if the guys were going to be there Friday night, I'd have to go on Wednesday, sign for barracks, tanks, ammo, and ranges. Then Sunday everybody would leave, and I'd be there until Wednesday of the next week clearing barracks, tanks, ammo, ranges. Eventually it got to be just too harsh, it was a lot of stress to handle, essentially learning how to be a cop in those first few years at the department, and then having to do the Guard for twelve weeks out of the year. When I left the Sheriff's department and got hired on at one of our local jurisdictions, I was only there for a year until the chief asked if I could leave the military. Not only was it getting harsh on my family, harsh on me, but it was also having an effect on our manpower at the department, and so after fifteen years in the military, I retired, five years shy of getting my retirement, because I wanted to focus on my career as a police officer."

"Did it bother you, not being able to potentially get two retirements?" I asked.

"Not really," he said, "and the reason it didn't bother me is because I really did want out. If I had wanted to stay in the military and be a lifer, then that would have been a different story. It was just time for me to move on, I wanted to do something else, and I had a family to consider."

"So, it was the right decision, in hindsight?"

"I think so, I think so," he repeated.

With two interviews down, I was starting to put together a clearer picture of the timeline of Charles' career between the military and the police force. In all, hearing about his upbringing, his parents, and his experiences in the military, it revealed a great deal about how he had become the man sitting in front of me. This strong, yet gentle individual who hid more pain behind his eyes than I could imagine at the time. As we were about to launch into our effort to discuss the major events in his career as an officer, I couldn't help but reflect, personally, on the jarring dichotomy which presented itself when comparing his life to mine. Charles' fifty-two years had been marked by hardship and distress, whereas my twenty-five to that point had been almost the exact opposite picture. Given the sacrifices he made for his community, his city, and his country, I almost felt guilty and selfish looking him in the eye, as I held the stark contrast of our two lives in the back of my mind. And everything that was to come, all the stories he would tell from his long career as a police officer, would reveal to me how much he truly suffered.

Chapter Two

"Life and death"

If there had been one subject matter from Charles' career that I was most intrigued to discuss with him, it had to have been one of the first themes which we decided together would feature prominently in his memoirs. That subject? Life and death. I was anxious to hear these stories from him, because according to Charles, these types of experiences as an officer had affected him so deeply, he told me, that he ended his career with an almost warped perspective on death in general, and I wanted to figure out how that had come about, both physically and mentally. I could only think of a few other occupations, members of the military to be sure, doctors and nurses, ambulance technicians, and maybe firefighters, where those persons are exposed to the fallout of violence, or become intimate with mortality, on a consistent basis.

"So, life and death, huh?" I began.

"Yeah, life and death. Sometimes it's difficult for people to understand what goes on in the average day of an officer, people sometimes have the impression that you don't see death and suffering very often, you know, that we're mostly sitting on our asses in our cars. But that couldn't be further from the truth. And you know, even in a city where the crime rate is low, a cop's life could still be in danger every day."

"Certainly," I said.

"So really, unless you've been in law enforcement or have a family member who has, it's hard for a regular citizen to understand what it's like to put your life on the line day after day on American streets," he declared.

"Well, what about people in the military, people who have been in war zones?"

"They would understand too, definitely, but being a cop is just a different experience from being in combat."

"How so?" I asked.

"Well, you see..." He pondered my question for a few seconds, and then continued.

"In the military you're part of a unit, and you follow orders, and a lot of the decisions are made for you. You have one role to play and that's what you do. War is different from being a police officer. When you're a police officer, you can't go out thinking it's a war zone, even though it may feel like it sometimes. You have to realize that as an officer, you live in the community and you're part of it, you're a servant to the public. You safeguard the general public from persons who engage in criminal wrongdoing, and you safeguard your own life from the criminals themselves, because a lot of them do want to harm you as well."

After another long pause, he finished his thought.

"So I'd say, being a soldier is less personal than being a cop is."

"That make sense," I responded. "Since police work is inherently about serving and protecting the community, it makes the consequences of your actions all the more real."

"Yep."

We were back in my apartment, and this was the third Thursday in a row we had met for an interview. Progress was good so far, and at this point, Charles was beginning to get excited about the project, and that certainly caused me to feel good, personally. I was happy that he was happy.

I got up from my seat and quickly put on some coffee for myself, then went back over to get us started while it was brewing.

"So, how about we get right to it?" I asked.

"Okay, let's do it," he replied.

I flipped open my journal and glanced at the brief list of questions I had written down for myself to ask him. A routine we had developed for the interviews was to first have a phone call earlier in the week, where we would discuss and then agree upon the stories we would be recording in the next session. Charles would also provide me with a short description of each of the stories he wanted to tell, and we would come up with a temporary title for each story, so we could reference it later, if necessary. For this session, however, the content of our routine call had simply been to confirm that we were both indeed, free to meet on that Thursday. He had assured me that we would have plenty to talk about on the subject of life and death, which, unfortunately, was not surprising.

"So, when you're talking about life and death from the perspective of a police officer, you're mostly talking about murders and people being seriously and mortally injured, but you're also talking about those times when you're faced with a life-threatening situation on the job, or you have to make a life or death decision. Does that sound accurate?" I queried.

"That's all correct, yes."

"Can you tell me about some of the times in your career where you faced some of those types of decisions, then?"

"Of course."

Charles shifted in his chair and cleared his throat. After thinking for a few seconds, he nodded to himself and looked up at me.

"So, we can start with this one, this is a big one. This was on a night, when I was patrolling one of the tougher parts of the city, and, there are some apartment complexes in this area that were always on our radar, because there are a lot of known criminals who lived in them. And so, let me describe the scene for you really quick."

"Okay."

"So, the apartment complexes are on one side of the street, and there's a traffic light nearby, and a mini-mart drive-thru kind of place on the other side on one corner, and adjacent to it on the same side of the street was a Church of Christ, or a Baptist Church I think, can't remember exactly. And on the one corner with the church, there was a brick sign, you know, where the church puts letters inside to spell out messages for the community."

"Right."

"The sign came up about five feet off the ground at two angles, just a big rectangular sign facing out to the street. And so, we got a call for a B and E in progress, breaking and entering at the drive thru, and we respond, me and two other cops who showed up with me. And there was a little park there too, right next to the place that had just gotten burglarized, and so we were checking that area after we had cleared the drive thru and checked it out completely. The mini-mart had been broken into, but it had been closed at the time of the robbery, so there hadn't been anyone inside to watch the store. So, we cleared the place, and then we went back out on the street to clear the surrounding streets."

"That's standard protocol for a B and E?"

"Yep, that's right. Since the robbery had occurred so recently, there was still a good chance that the suspects were still in the area, so we decided to fan out a few blocks. My fellow officers went north, out towards one of the main streets, and I went the other way towards the church, and pretty soon I encountered a guy out walking about two blocks up from the drive thru. So, in order to figure out who he was, I pulled over to the side of the road by the church, so I basically turned into the next street up from the guy and had my car on the corner blocking his path."

"I take it you could tell there was something suspicious about this guy?" I asked.

"Pretty much, I mean it was late at night on a weekday, not a lot of people walking the streets in the first place at that time of night, had his hood down. So anyway, I pulled up in front of him, got out of my car, and this guy is just acting really weird. He's taking steps in one direction and then another, facing me, moving back and forth, and he's just really fidgety, you could tell something was up, his hands kept going down toward his legs and back up towards his chest, just fidgety. What I eventually figured out was that he was trying to keep my back turned away from the church. That will be important here in a minute."

"Okay."

"So I'm trying to deal with him, asking him to identify himself, and what he's doing out so late at night, but he's not helping, he's not saying a word. So I'm finally just done with the antics, I've had enough, so I decide to step in and grab him. I spin him around and tell him to put his hands onto my car so I can search him. And that's when it happens."

"What happens?"

"He had a gun with him, and he tried to pull it on me."

"Damn."

"Yeah, really. So, his right hand went to his waistband to grab his gun, and I see that, and my hand goes on top of his automatically. At this time, I could push him away and we could draw, and we could shoot it out within two feet of each other, and I'd be justified if I had killed him. But then again, I probably would have gotten hit too, probably would have died right there too if that happened. So obviously I don't do that, and I'm fighting with him over this gun, but here's the even crazier part."

"What?"

"So, what I didn't know was that there were three other guys who were doing the break-in with him, all armed, one with a shotgun and two with pistols, and they had been hiding near the church, or in the church, don't know exactly, and when they saw me pull their guy over, you know, they decided to come over to help him out. And so they were actually hiding behind that brick wall sign, the church sign I was telling you about, and they were waiting and were about to come over to shoot me in the back! That's why he had kept me turned away from that spot, why he was being erratic with his movements, because he didn't want me to face that direction and see them coming. He was trying to maneuver me so my back would stay turned to the church."

"Wow, I can't believe that..."

"I know! So now, I'm in the middle of a fight with him over his gun, and I had been just able to yell 'Gun!' on my radio to alert the other officers. It was about a half a minute into the struggle when I saw the other three guys coming out of the corner of my eye, they're about fifty feet away, but thankfully, my fellow officers were just right around the corner and had their sirens blaring, which probably scared those guys off before they could try and come over and shoot me and save their buddy. So those three took off running away from us and into this apartment complex, which I think was where they probably lived. The other officers decided not to pursue them and instead come to my aid and deal with the immediate threat, which was the guy who had tried to pull his gun on me."

"Probably a good idea."

"Uh huh. At that point, I'm still engaged with the suspect and we were wrestling, we were banging up against my car, and I'm trying to decide what to do, you know? I didn't want to kill him, so I'm like, 'alright fuck you dude, I'm taking your fucking gun,' so I push him to the ground and start beating his hand on the curb, and finally it knocks loose, and one of my partners who had just arrived gets to it and grabs it, tosses it on the grass, and he gets down with me and we're fighting with this guy, and we finally get him cuffed."

I shook my head.

"Well at least it was a happy ending."

"That was probably the best outcome in that situation, for sure. Then what happened next was, we took the suspect into custody and he talked to the detectives, and he *actually* said that his intent was to kill me, or for one his buddies to kill me when I had my back turned. I mean he straight out said it, so they ended up charging him with that too, and they didn't get but one of the other guys involved, and they got charges pressed against him too. And I went down to the gun range over at our police academy, and test fired that gun and it shot right away. It was loaded and ready to go, one in the chamber."

"Some people really don't care if they shoot a cop, do they?"

"Oh yeah, it's true. Some people are going out and committing crimes, and just waiting for us to respond so they can take one of us down. I mean, for some people at least. For other people, it's a fight or flight response. They happen to have a gun on them, and sometimes they're remorseful after if they've taken an officer's life. But some people do actually hate cops with all their being and want to see us dead, but we'll get into that later."

"Yeah, definitely."

"And so what happened with this guy was, right, he was trying to make his decision at the time, was he going to let his friends shoot me or was he going to shoot me, because his hands were going all over the place"

"Oh yeah, that's right, that's why he was acting so weird."

"Yep that's why he was so fidgety, because he was trying to decide what he wanted to do. See, he was pretty much controlling that situation, he could have made a fateful decision as to what would happen between him and I. He could have pulled his gun as I was getting out of my car and I wouldn't even have had the chance to get a hand on my weapon. Thankfully he didn't do that, but here's the other thing I have to say about situations like this. And this is important. People have to understand that use of deadly force for a cop is an absolute, last resort."

I nodded. "Nobody wants to kill anybody."

"Absolutely. Nobody wants to get shot, get killed, get stabbed. So, you try to resolve situations like this, in the heat of the moment of course, but you try to resolve them with the least amount of violence as possible. Like I said, I could have drawn my gun on him when I saw him reaching for his gun, and we could have shot each other right there within arms-length of each other, but what would that have solved?"

"Nothing."

"Nothing at all. So, I decided that it wasn't going to happen, that we weren't going to shoot each other, that I would go home to my family safe and he would be safe too, that way he could have an opportunity to turn his life around if he wanted to, instead of losing his life right there. So, to that effect, when we're struggling with the gun, I had to pull out all my moves, had to push him against the car, throw him against the ground, trying my best to disarm him, and then whatever happened after that was in God's hands at that point. If I hadn't taken aggressive action against him in that moment, then it probably would have ended badly for both of us, but I was going to try my best to keep him, and myself, alive."

"That's a lot to think about in your head in the span of about three seconds," I said.

"You know, it is, but those are decisions that you have to make as an officer. And I mean, here's something I want people to know. One thing I want them to know is just how ordinary of a person I am. At the end of the day, I'm just a regular guy who wants to come home to his wife and kids. I have an obligation to my family to come home safe every night, and I'm doing this job to feed them, to keep a roof over their heads and food on the table. There aren't that many jobs on American soil where you fear for your life on a daily basis, but I chose this career, I chose to serve and protect the public, and it's not an easy life. I know people think that all cops are evil and that we're out to get you, but that's not the truth at all."

"You're just a regular guy."

"I'm just a normal guy, seriously. I'm not God, I'm not supposed to make decisions about whether people live or die. I have the right to defend life, of course, whether it's somebody else's or whether it's mine. And in that situation, I defended my life and his life, because I didn't want to die, or him to die, over breaking into a stupid convenience store for lottery tickets, some cigarettes and a little bit of cash."

That statement shocked me, for reasons I couldn't really articulate too well in the moment.

"Well when you put it like that..." I had a to pause for a second to gather my thoughts. "It crazy to think how many lives are lost over stupid stuff like a robbing a convenience store."

"Exactly. It's a depressing thought, it sure is. And so, that obligation to respect life and protect the sanctity of human life runs deeper than you might think. Cops just can't go running around and saying you know, 'hey I really want to shoot somebody today.' Those aren't good cops, those are the guys who let the power get to their heads. You have an obligation to the community, to yourself, and to those people you're going to take into custody, because you're liable for those people, and that decision is the biggest decision you will ever make. Do I want to be the cause of this person's death, and you know, deal with it in my head for the rest of my life? If I had shot him, that would be something I'd have to deal with forever, I would probably ask myself over and over again, did he have to die over that? What could I have done differently?"

To me, this was just something that I couldn't imagine myself, much less every single citizen in America, having to deal with on a daily basis at their employment. What I mean by referencing 'every single citizen' is merely the fact of the general public passing judgment so easily on the actions of the police in the heat of the moment. It kind of got me fired up during our discussion, I'll admit.

People have the audacity to put themselves in a police officer's shoes and second guess their actions, when those same people don't even know what they would do in a similar situation, and maybe haven't even thought about it? I'm not unrealistic about the problem of police brutality by any means, but I'll confess that talking to someone like Charles probably made me a bit biased in my judgement. There are definitely cops out there who are doing the job for the wrong reasons, but I think it's a bit of a stretch to say that those examples outnumber the examples of cops who are out there to do good. I have to believe that the majority of the police are just like Charles. Just regular people doing a job, which just so happens to be fraught with danger and life and death decisions.

Charles had continued talking while I was thinking about all this.

"And this goes back to what we have our weapon for, the reason we carry around a weapon with the potential to inflict deadly harm. The reason you have that gun is to defend your own life, or somebody else's. And you have to make that decision. In a split second, and people say 'well, why didn't you shoot him in the leg?' Well you know, I've got one second to decide what I need to do, I've got all the emotions running through me about how I might take someone's life over a stupid run, and how it might be necessary or it might not be necessary. I don't necessarily have time to think about aiming and shooting somebody in the leg."

"Not only that, but cops can get sued too, right, I mean there's liability involved." I might not have been knowledgeable about the job of a police officer before I met Charles, but that much I did know, just from hearing and reading the news.

He nodded affirmatively.

"You've got wrongful death suits, you got libel suits, you injure somebody, and now he says he walks with a gimp for the rest of his life, and you have to pay him for that, even though he was the one committing a crime! And so here, let's just add more on to the shoulders of these guys who we trust to carry guns, okay? Now we're going to tell a cop that anything you do, you could be sued for it, so keep that in mind when you're making out there making runs and having encounters with people who want to kill you..."

A question I had written down in my notes which I thought of while we were talking was about the legal complications surrounding police action. Something Charles had always told me in our conversations was that he was lucky that he had made it twenty years on the job without getting sued. So, I made a point of asking him about that, because I wanted to hear his thoughts on the subject.

"Do you think that this might be a weakness in our criminal justice system then? Do you think there should be set-in-stone limitations on the legal action that can be taken against the police? And you know, smart limitations, not so that the police are immune from prosecution, but just enough that they aren't hampered from doing their jobs effectively?"

"Yeah, you can have smart limitations, definitely, you know, as long as you're not denying someone their constitutional rights. That's the thing too, is that there's a difference between an effective police force and one which could go all Big Brother on you. You know me, I love the constitution, I carry a pocket copy of it wherever I go. So, I want cops to be able to do their job, but the rights of U.S. citizens are still very important."

"That's something we're still working on as a society, I guess."

"And we have to keep working on it, it's important to keep working on it, in this grand experiment we call America. But as far as the liability for cops goes, I think circumstances have to dictate what happens. If that person creates a situation in which he got injured, how can he sue somebody for stopping him from committing a crime, especially in a situation where his intention was to kill me?"

"I'd be interested to research more into what the statutes and laws currently on the books say about those situations," I said.

"Go for it, man. As a start I'd tell you to look up a judgement in the Supreme Court called Tennessee v. Garner."

"Okay."

"Tennessee versus Garner says that you can shoot a felon in the back, not if you have reasonable doubt, but if you have a reason to believe that they are going to go cause damage, injury or loss of life, because they have already done so. So, if some guy has just committed a murder and he's going around shooting people, and you're on the scene and you see him running away from you, you can take him out because of the exigent circumstances."

"I think I'm actually familiar with that case," I responded.

I did look up at that case, and the details were exactly as he described. I had personally developed an interest in constitutional law during my academic career, beginning when I was pursuing my undergraduate degree in political science, and Charles' devotion to the constitution was one of the things I liked about him. Not only that, but he was, in general, politically in the middle-ground, leaning conservative most of the time if he had to choose, but what I also liked about him in that respect was that he didn't get caught up in the extreme rhetoric that the two sides of our political system often peddled on television and in the news. He was smarter than that, and, what was more, he was an empathetic man, because he knew what it was like out in the real world. He knew how hard life could be, he was aware of the problems that regular Americans faced, because he had lived some of those hardships himself, and been exposed to the rest through all the people he met as an officer.

    We took a break after that first story. My coffee was done brewing, and so I got up and poured myself a cup. Charles wasn't a coffee drinker, as he preferred nicotine for his drug of choice, so he went outside on my balcony and smoked. This would end up being another routine we repeated each time he came over to my apartment for an interview. We would complete one or two recordings, and he would take a smoke break in between sessions, and sometimes we would order a pizza to have for lunch as well.

    When Charles came back inside, I was already sitting down at the dining room table, ready to get going again, and so he hung up his coat and put his cigarettes down on the small, oak end table which I had placed for him near the sliding door that opened to the balcony, and we started up another recording.

    "So, another time, I was also doing a patrol up on the north side of the city, and it was night time. We had a run, a possible B and E in progress of a bar in the area, well it was more of a club really, kind of a hole in the wall nightclub. We were very familiar with this place because we used to make runs there all the time, the establishment was borderline losing their license because they were serving minors, they were selling drugs out of there, it was just a shady place in general."

"Had anything violent occurred there in the past, or was it just, you know, a place where there was a lot of criminal activity?" I asked.

"Yes, there were violent crimes committed there, a couple murders if I remember correctly. Just a run of the mill drug habitat. So anyway, we started to pull into the area, it was me and another car, and as we pulled up to where this bar was located, and as I'm pulling around the corner to park, a guy comes busting out of the door with a strong box with the cash in it, and like a mechanic screwdriver in his hand, you know, one of those one's that's like a foot and a half long, two feet long."

I almost laughed a little at the picture which I had created in my head. It evoked an image of a hapless burglar often portrayed in the movies.

"Don't know how he didn't see or hear you guys coming, or didn't at least go out the back door," I commented.

Charles shook his head. "Couldn't tell you. So off he runs, he bolts across the street to cut through a neighborhood and try and lose us, and so at this point we both get out of our cars and the foot pursuit is on. We're chasing him on foot, breathing hard, and we go around the corner to another street, and he tries to start cutting through backyards. Big mistake. He went along this one house, and behind this house was like one of those big partitions, just a big, twelve-foot cement wall that served as a partition between two properties, with high fences on both sides as well. So, he had boxed himself in, and when he tried to double back down the driveway he met up with me. I had been hot on his trail, so I'm at the end of the driveway, flashlight on him, gun drawn, and he's got that screwdriver up in the air pointed toward me, in a stabbing position."

"Bad move."

"Yeah, never raise something that's two feet long and made of metal at an officer, that's for sure. And so at first I tell him, 'Drop the weapon and get on the ground!' But for some reason he keeps moving towards me, still has the screwdriver in a threatening position. I hold my ground for a few seconds but I'm trying to give him as much leeway as I can, so I start backing up a little too. And he keeps coming, but I'm just telling him, 'Drop the weapon and get on the ground,' and after that, after he doesn't show any signs of stopping his advance, I tell him 'I don't want to shoot you man, you're gonna die, two more steps it's not fucking worth it, you need to fucking stop.' But he continues to advance toward me, isn't really listening to what I'm saying, and at that point I've got three-quarters of the pressure pulled on that trigger and I'm still yelling at him 'Just stop man, drop the weapon, it's not worth dying!'"

Now at this point, I have to mention, I didn't know whether Charles had actually killed anybody during his career. That wasn't something we had talked about yet, interestingly enough. So, during this story in particular, I was almost on the edge of my seat listening to him, because it seemed like this would be the kind of situation where he would have had little choice but to shoot the guy.

Charles continued.

"Then all of the sudden, it was like his feet hit a glue trap. He stopped dead, fell flat on his face and dropped everything, and put his hands out. A half a second away from being dead, a half a second, because I couldn't afford to give him any more time or space. I was just telling him 'Stop dude, just drop the weapon,' but he kept on coming."

My jaw dropped. I had not expected that ending at all.

"How close was he from you when he stopped?"

"Less than ten feet. I guess it just hit his brain at the last second, because I was telling him, you know, 'It's not worth dying over man, just drop the weapon and get down on the ground.' And if I would have pulled the trigger, it probably would have been a shot that whizzed right over him as he fell, that's how close we were. It was just a matter of giving him as much time to make the right decision, he had the screwdriver up over his head in the offensive position to hit me with it, and I'm thinking 'How much can I give him, how much can I give him, how much can I give him?'"

"So there's two people who need to make decisions about life and death in this scenario, him and you. The suspect and the officer," I remarked.

"That's right. You give them as much time as you can, but then sometimes it will get to the point where you say, 'fuck, I can't give you any more time, sorry dude,' you know, because you're telling him the whole way, 'just stop, just stop man.' And if they don't comply, and you've given them ample opportunity to do so, it's 'sorry about your luck' at that point. You know, I know what his intentions are, he's just committed a robbery and he's in that flee or fight mode, and he couldn't flee, because there was a twelve-foot cinder block wall blocking his path, so it was fight, and it was on."

I still couldn't believe that the guy had just stopped.

"Absolutely unreal. I mean, he just must have had something click in his head," I said.

"That's really what it looked like, man, I almost couldn't believe it myself. He was almost on me, and it literally looked like his feet glued themselves to the driveway. He just stopped dead in his tracks, and fell flat on the ground, hands out front."

"Dropped the lockbox?"

"Dropped everything, the screwdriver, he looked like Superman, like he was flying on the ground. A half a second away from dying. And I was telling him after he went to the ground, I said 'Thank you for complying, there's probably a hundred bucks in that box, it wasn't worth dying over, man.' And I guess I finally got through to him, I told him three times, 'You're gonna die, it's not worth it, get on the fucking ground.'"

"That's crazy. Wonder what happened to him."

"Couldn't tell you, but hopefully he's in a better place in life now. It's been awhile since that happened."

I nodded my head and then looked down at the recorder. It seemed like a natural place to end the recording, but I knew we had at least a couple more stories to cover under the theme of 'life and death,' so I kept the dialogue going.

"Well, so I think you told me you had one about a bank robbery, right? Do you remember which one that was?"

"Yeah I remember that one, let's do it," he said.

"Alright, go ahead, we're still recording."

Charles looked up at the ceiling as he was figuring out how to begin, and I took a sip of my coffee.

"So, one day we had a bank robbery at a local credit union, but the suspect had gotten away, and we had brought in a dog to search for him, but the dog lost track of the guy one block over in a back street behind the bank. Doing a little detective work based on this fact, we decided that he must be parking a car on the back street and getting away that way, which was why the dog lost his scent. And so that was the next plan of action for catching the guy if it should occur again, because bank robbers usually get cocky is they pull off one successful heist, usually they'll try another one sooner or later."

"Makes sense," I said.

"Well so sure enough, there it goes again, bank robbery in progress comes over on the radio, at the same credit union no less, and so another officer and I are responding, he heads to the bank itself and I head to the back streets behind it to have a look around. As I'm pulling into one of those back streets, I see the suspect running to his van, parked on a street which was headed toward one of the outbound roads. So I cut his van off with my car, blocking him into the parking space he was in."

"Got there just in time then."

"Yep, the plan worked. So, this was right as he was about to back out, I got him blocked in, I got my door open, standing over my car, yelling at him, 'Let me see your hands, let me see your hands.' I was assuming that he was armed, it had been implied he had been armed in the last robbery, but a weapon hadn't been seen by the people at the bank this time, so we actually had no clue. So it's a 'better safe than sorry' thing for me, I'm assuming he's armed and proceeding with caution, I continue to move forward to the car in a defensive position with my weapon pointed at him, and I'm yelling to see his hands. After about fifteen seconds probably, he puts his hands up, I can see them up through the car, and so I start to make my approach to make the arrest."

"I'm already nervous for you and I don't even know what's going to happen," I said.

"Yeah man, as an officer you never know what you're going to be walking into in a given situation. Never know if you're going to get ambushed, or somebody has a knife on them, that's why it's a dangerous job. And that leads me to what happened next, so, right when I get up near to his window, his right hand dropped between the front seat and the passenger seat in a quick manner. At this point, I'm already aimed center mass at him, yelling at him, almost to the point where I'm asking him not to pull anything, like please, 'show me your hands man, don't do anything stupid,' but he doesn't listen, and he comes up very quickly with an object in his hand and points it right at me."

"No way, seriously?"

"Really stupid decision on his part, I know. But for me, the pressure is on, in a split second all of the threatening thoughts are going through your head, like 'What is the object, can I immediately tell what it is, can he hurt me,' and so in that split second I made the decision that what he had couldn't harm me, even though, you know, it was dark in color and pointed in my direction, but he's trying to get me to pull the trigger, yelling 'Shoot me motherfucker!'"

"Yeah I was about to say, seems like this guy had a death wish."

"He probably did, and you know, death by cop is a common way people try to commit suicide, even though I don't know if that was his motivation for wanting to get shot or not, he definitely knew he was facing multiple counts of armed robbery. But anyway, thankfully the object was just a hairbrush, just a plain old hairbrush, and I could see that it was a hairbrush when had pulled it up from between the seats, even though he had done it in a relatively quick motion, I had seen the brush part and saw that what he was pointing at me was just the end of it, the handle."

I laughed a little when he said that, mostly out of relief that there hadn't actually been a weapon involved.

"And so once I had ascertained that he wasn't a threat to me, I pulled him out of the car, but he kind of pushed back on me when he got out, so we tussled on the ground for a few seconds, me trying to get his hands behind his back so I can cuff him, and then backup finally shows up, and they whisk him away."

"Just another situation where someone could have died though."

"Yep, if I hadn't had the awareness to recognize that he didn't actually have a gun, I could have easily shot him right there. You know, maybe I didn't get enough sleep the night before and I wasn't as sharp mentally or physically as I usually was, things could have easily been different. There's a fine line there between life and death in those types of situations, and cops walk it every day."

I ended the recording there, knowing that Charles would want to go outside for a smoke break again, and this time I joined him, and he offered me a cigarette and I accepted. Usually when we went out to the balcony, we would just sit out there, talk about life, and enjoy the view. I would ask him about his kids, and he would ask me about school and work. We were starting to get to know each other's lives pretty well by that point.

Back inside, he decided on one more story to tell, and this one was an important one.

"Okay, whenever you're ready," I said.

"So, this was a hot summer's night, I remember it was hot because I had just been sweating like crazy since the start of the shift, even with the AC on full blast. Me and another officer were responding to a call on the west side of town, a domestic incident in progress, we had one officer on the scene already, and another officer and myself were on the way. This is early in my career, and we were both new cops on the scene, had only been on my own something like one and a half, two months maybe."

"Got it."

"So what we were dealing with here, was an apartment complex that had a driveway that went up a hill, and in front of it there was a big grassy slope. We approached up the hill, not knowing what we were walking into, could have never known what we were walking into in this case."

"Always dealing with unknowns."

"Always, especially with domestic violence runs. So we get to the top of the hill and immediately see the other officer in the back corner of the building with the suspect, who's wearing nothing but a pair of shorts and holding two, really, really big butcher knives. This was someone I had dealt with a few times already, even though I was just a young cop, and so this guy recognizes me automatically as we're approaching, and he yells at me and says "I'm not going back to prison, Bell, I'm not going back to fucking prison!""

"Wow, so it's a little bit personal now?"

"You could say that, I had talked with the guy before on a couple occasions, and so I knew him just well enough that I kind of cared about what happened to him, didn't want him to get hurt. So I tell him, I said 'Look man, let's just talk about this and we'll work something out okay, it's probably not that big a deal, let's see what's happening.' And he was like 'No, no way man, I'm not going back.' And this had all sprung from an altercation with his niece who had just called us, he had had a prior for domestic violence, don't know who he had been violent with, and I can only guess at the details of the relationship with his niece."

"Right."

"So, he had the two knives, and as we're talking with him we continue to get closer. We try to stay about twenty-one feet away from a potential assailant who is armed with a bladed weapon, that's the rule, because within twenty-one feet a person who is armed with a knife can close that distance and stab you before you can draw your gun and defend yourself. So, I'm trying to talk to him, and at this point we're way past the twenty-one foot rule, and as me and the other officer are talking to him, he turns and faces me, knowing how close we're getting, and he starts coming toward me with the knife, swinging them in the air, at which point you know I probably should have shot him, it would have been justified, there were weapons involved and an imminent threat on my life."

"So why didn't you?"

"Well, you know, being young it gave me a little pause. I had decided early on in my training that I didn't want to start my career out that way, because they always warned us that as inexperienced officers, we might have a tendency to be a little trigger-happy, but I always felt that it was better to first find a way to talk things through with people. So due to my training there's a million things going through my head in that moment when he starts closing in on me, about justification and civil suits, and knowing who this guy was, and everything else that goes through a cop's brain in a life threatening situation, and at this point he's closed the gap even further to about ten feet, and I have my weapon trained on him but I'm still talking to him, telling him to put the knives down so we can talk it out, and I keep saying it. 'We'll talk it out man, let's talk it out.' 'Just put the knives on the ground and we'll figure this out,' but he would just keep saying 'No, fuck you man, fuck you.'"

"He really, really didn't want to go back to prison."

"It seemed that way, his mind was probably already made up to be honest, but I still tried to talk him down from the ledge. So he keeps advancing and at a certain junction, we decide to just back away, he hasn't made an earnest rush toward any of us yet, he was just kind of daring us to shoot, not attacking but not staying far away from us either. The other officers and I, we start backing down the driveway as he continues to advance. He backs us down to the street, and now there's people starting to show up and peak out their windows and doors to watch what's happening. And eventually he gets us to the middle of the street. And this is a small street, there's cars parked on both sides, a little bar down on one end and a gas station further down, but the problem is that he's now surrounded on all sides by officers. So there aren't too many options in this situation, for him or for us. He's still making moves at us, trying to get us to shoot him, but not only do we *not want* to shoot him, but since we're all surrounding him nobody *can* shoot, because if we did we'd end up hitting each other."

"Yeah, definitely want to avoid friendly fire."

"Exactly. So, while this is going on we had called for more backup, and another officer brought out some equipment, so we could try and contain him, big shields and cans of mace and pepper spray, stuff like that. I had backed up to grab a shield and started to work back toward him, and I had another officer in front of me at about eleven o'clock, and so the suspect starts coming at us, but that's what we wanted him to do, because now we had the shields, so we could protect ourselves and try and take him down that way and potentially disarm him. And so we get to the point where there's probably four feet distance between him and me and my fellow officer, and for some unknown reason, he just stops out of the blue, and he turns to the other officer, who hadn't gotten himself a shield yet so he was basically unprotected, and not only that but he was backed up against a brick wall on the other side of the street."

"Oh no."

"But he had his gun out of course, so he wasn't completely unprotected. And so the guy turns to my fellow officer and says, 'Hey, you're a redneck motherfucker, you'll shoot me!' And he barrels full speed at the officer, who had no choice but to shoot him."

I had pretty much figured that someone was going to get shot, so I wasn't as shocked by that detail as I was by the comment the assailant had made.

"So the only reason why he had been able to get off a shot was because the grassy hill was behind suspect when he was attacking, so the officer was clear of us to fire, but remember, he was backed against the wall of a building too, so the only option he had unfortunately was to shoot the guy, or it was death by butcher knife. The shot was true, hit him in the chest area, the suspect fell to the ground and dropped the knives, and then everything basically went into slow motion at that point."

"I can imagine..."

"Every breath this guy takes, a fountain of blood would come up out of his chest and then roll down onto the ground. We approached, got the knives out of the way, and we actually had a medic who had just arrived at the scene on standby, so after we searched his body we got him loaded up and cuffed to the gurney as quickly as we could. So he's headed off to the hospital, and the officer who shot him had to head down to the detective's office to give his statement, which is never a pleasant experience. This is where they either read you your Miranda rights or Garrity rights depending on the nature of the situation, and the officer has to go through the entire sequence with the detectives, they have to explain in great detail exactly what was going on and what had happened."

"As with any officer-related shooting, right?"

"That's correct. But back to the crime scene. So, at this point my nerves are shot, I was a young officer, and the guy who had shot the suspect happened to be my friend, and so my friend wasn't with me, didn't know what was going to happen to him, and we we're out there surrounding the area so the crime scene could be processed without disruption. All of the sudden I realize that a pretty large crowd had built up on the street and the surrounding streets to watch us work. Then about an hour later the local news shows up, and their usual first step is to interview one of the bystanders to get their opinion on what happened, and this guy they interview, he was going on about how the guy we had just shot was his cellmate at the justice center, and so he was saying 'He was my celly at the JC, and Bell killed him!'"

"Wait, what?"

"I know, right, that was the kicker, this one guy who they interview, who probably didn't even see what had happened in the first place, said my name directly on camera even though it hadn't been me. So the press is writing down names, they don't even bother asking us first about the details before they put out the first round of news coverage, and so they put someone on live television saying that it was me who had pulled the trigger, when it was actually my fellow officer. So that was me getting falsely accused of shooting a member of the community, and I got some hate for that until people finally heard, first of all, that the guy lived, and second that it actually hadn't been me. But then of course, the officer who had actually shot him, that was just a bad situation, there was nothing else he could have done."

"No, I mean, those are the kinds of situations that you never want to be in as an officer, and it happens to him on his first few months on the job, that's pretty crazy," I commented.

"It affected him a lot, it did, obviously he was innocent of any crime, but shooting someone in a situation like that certainly is something a cop would definitely prefer not to have on their record."

"For sure, yeah."

"So, once this guy gets out of the hospital, he goes to jail for the domestic incident and also for the attempted murder of an officer, and subsequently he gets probation or something, and does very little time, I can't remember why. And when he gets out, now he's making threats against that officer and all of us when we make runs to his place several more times, and eventually he gets caught up on more charges and goes back to prison."

"Damn, got what he deserved I guess. Didn't seem like the most quality human being to begin with, anyway," I said.

"I mean, yes and no. There are some people who deserve prison and some people who don't. Some people you can tell if they've just made a big mistake or a series of mistakes that they couldn't necessarily stop themselves from doing, and other guys, there are other guys who are straight up evil or they just don't care who they hurt and don't care about the consequences of their actions. It's tough to differentiate sometimes, though."

We ended the session soon after he completed his monologue. That last story had been one of the defining experiences in Charles' career, and so I was glad we were able to fully flesh out all the details. Those details also made me respect him even more as an individual, mostly because of the notion that even at such an early stage in his career as an officer, he was already mindful of the consequences of his actions. But of course, as the previous account of his fellow officer indicated, sometimes cops don't get to control their actions, much less the consequences.

Chapter Three

"Send in the dolphins!"

    A couple of weeks passed before our next interview, as I had called Charles on Wednesday of the next week and asked if we could skip the next day's meeting, due to the fact I was suffering from flu-like symptoms, and didn't want to get him sick. Charles agreed, and thought it would be best for me to get some rest, and he would appreciate some rest himself, in any case, he said. So, we did skip that Thursday, and would meet on the following Thursday, and I spent the interim days getting well, catching up on sleep, doing homework, and also doing some work on our project as well. I ended up putting together a rough outline of what Charles and I would be discussing over the next month or so.

    During this session, we decided to cover some of the calls Charles had responded to during his career involving mental illness in his community. I prompted our first conversation with a question.

    "So, you probably had a hundred of these kinds of cases during your career, involving people with mental illness or people with physical or mental disabilities?"

    "Of course, and you know, that was just another part of being a servant to the community. It means you deal with *everyone* in the community, you have to be there whenever there's a crisis, whether it's mental health or otherwise. Some people might feel uncomfortable encountering a person with a major mental illness, but we have to as officers, it's part of our job. Those were common occurrences for us, and mental health was a big issue in our community. There were eight halfway houses within the city limits, and you could find all kinds of people in them. People thinking they're being controlled through the television, people throwing things at the walls for no reason, people having hallucinations and visions, just any kind of mental health problem you could dream of, we probably saw it."

"I'm sure, yeah."

I opened up my journal and found where I had taken down a few notes in preparation for this particular interview.

"So, I wrote down the descriptions of those stories you told me about on the phone, there were three of them I think."

"Okay."

I handed him the notebook.

"Go ahead and look over those real quick and see which one you want to start with first, hopefully you can read my handwriting."

"Can't be worse than mine, my friend."

He adjusted his glasses and looked over what I written.

"Okay, yeah those are good ones. Well, let's do the shotgun one first, that was pretty intense."

"Alright, sounds good."

Charles cleared his throat, and I started the recording.

"So, for this one, we responded to a call, we had to go see a mentally-disturbed person who we knew about, it was a mother and son who lived together in an apartment, and the son was mentally ill. This was an adult, the son was, someone who hadn't ever broken the law, but someone who we had been called to investigate and check on beforehand on a few occasions. This was someone who we also knew, through information we had gathered previously from their case worker, could be violent. So, we get to the apartment complex, and we see the individual's mother coming down the stairs, and we see that she's got a gun. She's not pointing it at us, yet, she kind of has it held downward, pointed downward, and it's a big gun, it's a shotgun."

"How many officers were there?" I asked.

"There were four of us who responded. And once we had observed that she had a weapon, the two lead officers drew their guns and were on their guard, and me and another officer were a few feet back, still near our cars, so we backed off another few feet to take cover."

"I'm sure it's difficult to figure out what to do in this kind of situation, you've got to be careful I guess," I commented.

Charles shook his head affirmatively. "Yeah, you've got to be careful, got to be delicate, because again, nobody wants there to be loss of life, and you're first goal if there is a weapon is to try and resolve the situation and try and have it not end in a shootout. So, I've got my twelve-gauge with me, and I'm kneeling next to my car in a defensive position. We hadn't even seen the son yet, the guy we had been called to check on, but we didn't think he was armed, although we didn't know where he was at that point. But obviously his mother was armed, and at a certain point in the standoff she ended up pointing the gun up at us, and the shot gun is racked, and she says she's going to kill us, because she's tired of us coming for her son. So tensions are running high, for sure."

"But nobody had committed a crime up to that point, right, the mother or the son?"

"Nope, we were actually there on the behalf of Mobile Crisis, it's an organization concerned with mental illness patients in the city, and we were going on their behalf to come get this guy, because I guess they had decided that he needed to be taken to the hospital for a psych evaluation, for whatever reason. Maybe he had shown some warning signs of needing help or they discovered he wasn't taking his medication, and so since he had a history of violent outbursts, they needed our help to take him."

"Got it. So that was why were there four of you who came, why so many?" I asked.

"Well, so usually dispatch decides how many officers are needed, which is based on how many runs we've been on involving that particular person or a particular address in the past, and so with the combination of the person having a history of violence, us having dealt with him on prior occasions, and the recommendations from Mobile Crisis, we knew we were going to need as many people as possible to deal with a situation like this."

I nodded in understanding, and Charles continued.

"So, she's coming down the stairs form the apartment, yelling and screaming and waving a shotgun and threatening us, and I mean, we could have shot her as soon as she came down the stairs, but we're trying not to do that obviously."

"Why was she threatening to shoot everybody again?" I asked.

"Because she was tired of us trying to come and take her boy, which we hadn't ever done, as the police, but you know, I'm sure she had some mental health problems as well, and she might have been imagining things. So, for a couple minutes this was going on, she was yelling at us and waving and pointing her shotgun, and finally we decided to try and use an alternative measure to try and end the situation. We had just gotten tasers at this time, probably two weeks before this happened."

"What year was this?" I asked.

"This was early 2000's. The lead officer made the decision, and he brought his taser out and decided to use it to see if it worked, because we didn't know exactly what she was going to do. I had never deployed a taser in the field yet as of that time, and I don't think the lead officer had either. But anyway, so our lead officer uses the taser, and the gun drops out of her hands and she drops to the ground as the electricity is going through her, and we get over there and secure the weapon. So that got resolved quickly and quietly, the taser worked, but we still didn't know where the son was."

"Yeah that was my question, where was he when all this was happening?"

"Well, we assumed he was watching from a window or something, because as soon as she hits the ground, the son comes running out and decides to defend his mom's honor, and so he comes up to us and starts swinging at us and fighting. I had originally thought that two or three of us would be enough to subdue this guy, but after a few seconds it became clear that that wasn't going to be the case. So, I opened the slide of my shotgun and set it aside, went to help them out, and it ended up taking all four of us to get him in cuffs, had to put three sets on him to get his arms behind his back."

"I can't believe that, wow."

"I mean he was a grown man, and he was in that fight or flight mode to protect his mom, so he had a lot of fight in him, and he was angry at us and not thinking clearly."

"I guess so." I shook my head. "So this one got called in from his social worker then?" I asked.

"Exactly, she had called and asked us to go get him and take him to the hospital, which we had to do a lot, because the Mobile Crisis people are not capable of doing something like that, retrieval of a potentially violent individual. And it could have been for a number of reasons, that he hadn't seen his doctor in a while, maybe he wasn't taking his medication, and so if the case worker has identified that something needed to be done, or else somebody was going to get hurt, then that's when they call us. So we were responsible for getting him unharmed to the hospital, not to jail, he didn't go to jail, and he wasn't going to go to jail anyway unless you know, he injured someone severely or killed someone. But really all he did in that situation was fight us in defense of his mom, and none of us got hurt, so that's not something we were going to charge him for, that's something we would just forget about, we wouldn't charge a mentally ill person in a case like this."

"I mean it would have probably made things worse in his life, too," I remarked.

"It probably would have, you're right. If there's a crisis going on in somebody's life, we don't want to add to it if we can help it."

"I know I wouldn't feel good, you know, in my conscience, charging him with a crime."

"Exactly. It's the human thing to do."

I ended the recording there.

"That was a good one," I told Charles. "I wasn't aware previously of the role the police have in cases like that. I thought it was mostly citizens who called in when they know someone in their family or someone they know is in trouble, and would take care of that kind of situation privately."

"It is mostly, most of the time it is a simple civilian matter, but sometimes the case worker or someone in an organization like Mobile Crisis will call on people's behalf."

Again, this was another situation where I was learning something from talking to Charles, learning about situations that I hadn't been exposed to in my own life. This is not to say that I had been sheltered as a child, that my family didn't have our own problems, or that I didn't have my own personal struggles to deal with growing up. None of that is true. But what I will say that my upbringing and life experiences had been relatively utopian in comparison to the lives of the people Charles dealt with on a daily basis as a police officer. For me, listening to Charles and the narratives from his career was providing me with a view of our society I had not been regularly exposed to in my life up to that point.

His next story would be a welcome break from reality. Literally.

"So this one, this was when I was on the day shift, and I was responding to a civilian who had told dispatch that she was trapped in her apartment. I head over to the address and put my sirens on just in case, because I don't really know a whole lot about what might be going on, I didn't know this individual from any previous runs, and there wasn't much else to go on from her call other than that she was trapped and needed help."

"So, she locked herself in her apartment somehow?" I asked.

"No it wasn't that, it was something completely unexpected, but you'll find out. For these types of calls where you don't know a lot going in, you know, it could be trouble, or it could be a false alarm, and you hope there isn't anything really bad happening, but you're prepared for the worst anyway. So, I arrive, and I knock on the door and announce my presence, and right after I do that I hear her responding to me from inside, and she starts yelling and says "I can't make it to the door, I can't make it to the door!" And I respond and ask if she's hurt or if she's fallen down. And she says, 'No I'm standing on a chair and my apartment is filling up with water, and there's a shark trying to eat me!'"

I raised my eyebrows. Didn't see that coming.

"So I said 'What?' And she says back, 'They're trying to eat me and my whole apartment is full of water!'" Charles repeated.

"Obviously the apartment's not full of water, right?" I asked, just to be sure.

"Yeah, there's no water. And I didn't know coming into this situation that she was suffering from a mental illness, but that was becoming clear as the seconds went by. So at that point I really haven't figured out what I'm going to do yet, but I keep the dialogue going. I ask her, 'Can you come to the door then, can you make it to the door so I can let you out?' And she says, 'No, the sharks will get me.' So I'm thinking, 'What can I do to get her to come to the door,' I can't just leave of course, she called us so I have to resolve the situation. It was apparent that she was either on drugs or needed some help, so whatever the case was, I still had to talk her into coming to the door."

"Unbelievable. I really have no idea what I would have done," I said.

"Well, I had to think quickly," Charles said. "This lady is standing on top of her furniture thinking that there's an ocean with sharks in it inside of her apartment, what am I supposed to do? So, I kept talking to her for another minute or so while I'm thinking of what to do, and finally I get an idea."

"Let's hear it."

"So here's what I do, I tell her, 'Just hang on! What I'm going to do is send in our police dolphins, and they're going to attack the sharks and chase them away, so you can swim up to the door, does that sound good?' And she says, 'Huh, you got dolphins?' So in response to that, I had to really quickly go to my cellphone and look on the internet for sound effects, and so I pulled up a dolphin sounds video on YouTube, and turned the volume all the way up and held my phone close to the door so she could hear the video. And I guess she heard it loud and clear because almost right away she yelled back to me and said, 'Okay, okay, send in the dolphins!'" And so I just kept the video playing, kept playing the dolphin sounds, and after about a minute I hear her say, 'Okay I think it worked, I don't see the sharks anymore!' And a few seconds later she got to the door and opened it up for me."

I didn't know whether to laugh or just be absolutely amazed at the entire situation.

"So what, did she just imagine the dolphins fighting with the sharks and then the sharks swimming away?" I quipped.

"Well who knows, but I mean, whatever happened in there, it made her come to the door, so that was all I really cared about. Of course, there was no ocean water spilling out of her apartment or anything, and she wasn't wet either, but she was convinced that she had just come from the water and was thanking me for sending in the police dolphins to save her. So it was out with the K-9's and in with the K-Dolphins now!"

I smiled at that one.

"Really quick thinking on your part, though."

"Yeah it was, I was proud of myself for coming up with that one, had to think on my feet. Once I got her out into the hallway and started talking to her, I said, 'Hey, maybe we should go over to the hospital and have them go over your medications, and you can tell them all about what happened.' Well, she wasn't too keen on that idea, but then I said, 'Well you've been exposed to a lot of salt water, so they're probably going to want to check out your skin, and somehow she agreed to that, so I took her down to the psych ward from there."

"Nice job," I said.

"Thank you."

I stopped the recording and looked down at my notebook at our list. We only had one more story to cover for the day, and so I asked Charles if he wanted to take a smoke break before we got to the last down.

"I'm alright actually," he said, "let's do that one and then I'll take a smoke after and then I'll get out of here."

"Sounds good to me," I responded. I started a new recording, as Charles began his new monologue.

"So, on this last one, this involved an older lady who lived by herself, but she really shouldn't have been living by herself in the first place. We had received almost a hundred calls from her over a period of months, mostly about people in her house, she would think that there were people in her house, and when you'd get there you'd have to talk to her and say, 'I'll check in the closets for you and we'll get them out.' Well, there was nobody ever there but, if you get a call and someone is in distress and thinks they're in danger in their home, you have to go. I'll never forget the first time I went there to her apartment, she wanted us to go to the upstairs bedroom and check something out for her, and legitimately, this room was like a time capsule, hadn't been touched in what seemed like thirty years. There was just the thickest layer of dust over everything you could imagine, it was almost unsafe to breath in that room because of all the dust, and we had to be careful not to move too much of her stuff around because if we did, it probably would have created a dust cloud or something, it was crazy. The furniture was all really old, and there was one of those old phones where you spin the dial to call a number, you know what I'm talking about?"

"Yeah."

"And the other thing was, when I would go to her apartment, she would just follow me around, anywhere I went. It was kind of disturbing to be honest, because it kind of gave me the feeling that if I turned around at any moment she would stab me or something. And not only that but when she followed me around, sometimes she would laugh at me while I was searching the house for the people she was seeing. It was real weird, really creepy, always freaked me out whenever I had to go there."

"Well I mean you had to stop going there at some point, right? I mean, she couldn't keep wasting police time and resources forever," I wondered aloud.

"Yeah, so eventually we did have to take her away. One day I talked to her case worker, and she said that she was seeing these two teenage girls, who were supposedly herself and her sister who had died when they were that age, so those were like memories from her childhood coming back to haunt her. And this lady would tell me, 'Oh they're on my bed and they won't get off,' or 'They're in my living room talking about me and acting like they're not listening to me.' She lived in the downstairs and she just never went into her upstairs. Some of the times she would report strange lights and a hovering craft in her backyard, and then aliens trying to crawl up and come through her windows, so we would have to come and go through the house and make sure there weren't any grays, because she would call and say they were trying to abduct her on a weekly basis, and you would have to calm her down and tell her you were going to do extra patrols looking out for grays and flying saucers, which obviously we didn't do but, you know, we would make a couple passes by where she lived every hour or so just to make it seem like we were."

"Wow…"

"And so every time we had to make a run to her place we would have to call her nephew, who was her caretaker, but he lived in another state. So, the situation didn't get resolved for a while, but after four months of getting calls from her, the family decided it was best that she be placed under the care of the state. So that's how that story ended."

"The volume of calls that you got from her, though, I've never heard of anything like that before. I mean, I've never had to call the police in my lifetime, not even once," I said.

"Well, you're very fortunate then."

"I guess so," I responded.

Chapter Four

"Dead on arrival"

"Stop for a second, actually, let me take this call." Charles said.

I was just about to begin the recording of our latest meeting when his phone rang, and it was his wife, so Charles got up to answer it, and I remained seated. Meeting at my place was working out well, for a lot of reasons. It was easier for me and my schedule for him to come to me, and it worked with his schedule too, and furthermore, I suspected he enjoyed the brief respite from the daily trials of raising two teenaged boys at fifty-two years old.

After he hung up the phone with his wife, we settled back down at the dining room table and prepared for another interview. I had my laptop out, along with the recorder, my journal and a pen. I was actually doing homework on my computer during this interview, and whether Charles could tell or not that I wasn't completely focused on him, I didn't really know. But I don't think he really cared whether I was multi-tasking or not, just as long as the recorder was going so he could tell his stories. And he wouldn't have wanted me to fall behind in any of my classes. This was a serious time commitment for me, and he understood that.

"So, what were we going to work on today?" I asked out loud. We hadn't really come into this interview with a plan, as we had both been relatively busy that week. In my journal, I turned to the page with our list of themes, out of which we had already crossed off a few up to that point, and handed it to him. "Pick one for today, whatever you feel like doing."

He scrutinized the list.

"How about DOA's? We've got a lot of those stories to run through, and those are things people don't normally see on a daily basis."

"Works for me." I reached out to the recorder and hit the start button on a new recording. "Whenever you're ready."

"I'm ready," he said. "So, DOA. That stands for dead on arrival. On these types of runs, you can normally figure out what happened based on the scene, whether it's a potential crime scene or whether it's just a suicide. Just from your initial observations, there are usually tell-tale signs that make it clear what happened, how they died. Most of the time there's not a lot of mystery involved. You can see their pill bottle spilled out next to them, or you can tell by their age if they were sick or dying. A lot of times, it's what's behind the scenes, pun intended, that really gets you as an officer. If it's a suicide, sometimes there might be a note, but sometimes there's not, and if there is it is usually pretty vague, something that only the family or loved ones would understand if they read it. So, you walk out of suicide cases with a little bit of a bigger hole in your heart, because you don't know why it happened, or what could have been done. It's usually a younger person of course, which is even worse."

"I don't know how you did it, man, being exposed to so many of those," I said.

"Well, we'll talk about how it affected me later on, we could do a whole book on that, to be honest. But, on this particular day, I think I was about two years into being on the force at the time, we responded to a man who was shot, that was all we had, the parents had called and said that their kid had shot themselves. When we got there, the mom was already there, the dad was already there, and the victim was a young male, on the floor bleeding from his chest with an exit wound out of his back, blood coming out of his mouth, and he had shot himself straight through the heart. The parents were doing the best they could, but they didn't know how to do CPR, so they were begging us, me and another officer who responded with me, to do anything to help their son."

"God, that's fuckin' sad."

"I mean, this was probably one of the more traumatic events of my career, because I was young and impressionable, but I wanted to do something. I didn't want to just stand there. Now an older cop, an older cop probably would have stopped to think, because you don't know what this kid has, what diseases he might have, an older cop might have turned the parents down in a situation like that, might have said that there were too many health risks involved. So right there was a serious moral decision that I had to make."

"Whether to do CPR on him?"

"Yep, that was the decision I had in front of me. His parents are begging us to try and help, just to do anything, and that means potential exposure to me of bloodborne pathogens. So, me and the other officer were there, and I'm the one with training as a combat medic, so honestly, I didn't really think too much about the blood, my instincts just kind of kicked in, and I made the decision to start CPR myself before the medics arrive. For me it was a no-brainer, I was young, I wasn't thinking about the risks to my personal health, I was just thinking that a kid was dying on the floor and I had the ability to maybe keep him alive before help arrived."

"Good for you, good on you, man. I probably would have just frozen up."

"Well, thankfully, my fellow officer didn't, he was a more experienced officer, and he helped me as much as he could. First, we treated the kid for the sucking chest wound with basic first aid techniques, then we started with the CPR, so we could get some air pumped into his lungs. I did the breaths, and my partner did the compressions, and I was getting blood in my mouth doing this, of course, because with every compression, blood would come up and into his mouth and gurgle up into my mouth. After a couple of minutes, the paramedics got there, but by then it was too late. We did the best we could, but the kid just bled out too fast."

I was speechless. In a sense I had already known what the ending would be, given our theme for this chapter, but it didn't make it any less painful to hear about.

"That's terrible, man. You did what you could," I said.

"I did everything I could, everything in my power. So, once the paramedics called the time of death, I was in the kitchen with, you know, using dish soap to try and wash my mouth out, like that was going to help, but I didn't know that, I was just doing whatever I thought might work. Afterwards, I got lectured on blood exposure by my superiors, and then I had to go to the hospital, get some tests done, and start taking medication for HIV and get tested for Hepatitis. And it's a long time waiting for those results, it seemed like forever, and you're thinking in your head, should I have done that, should I have been selfish instead, but you know, I ask myself that question a lot, even to this day all these years later, and the answer always turns out to be yes. Because that's what you do, that's what you signed up for as an officer, you're there to save people's lives, not to turn people down when they need you the most, in the most dire place they've ever been."

"You have to be there for your community when they need you," I echoed.

"That's right. You never come first, if you don't make the decision to put yourself last, then you're not a very good cop. You know, I'm not trying to bad mouth other cops, because that is a tough decision obviously, but this job, those kinds of decisions just come with the territory. There's not a lot of room for selfishness, and that's why we signed up for the job. Being a cop is a job that, unfortunately, you know, probably fifty percent of the population just could not do. A cop doesn't know if, when they walk out of the door of their home and say goodbye to their wife and kids, that it might be the last time they see them again. Just no way of knowing. It's kind of eerie, gloomy feeling in the morning, when you walk out the door and head into work, because you're just facing the unknown, right, you just don't know what's going to happen. Suicides are rough."

I almost felt like I had to apologize to him for what he had been through.

"I almost feel bad making you have to remember all the details of these stories," I said. "It's like you're having to live them all over again."

"Well, these are the stories people have to hear, I want people to know what it's really like out there," he responded. "We had another suicide a few years later that was also a younger kid, and this kid was actually the stepson of one of my best friends from high school. He had hung himself over a girl, and I had to cut him down, being careful to be respectful to the body, and then I had to call my friend and let him know what had happened so he could call his wife. And they came to the scene and they were both hysterical when they saw their son's body, it was horrible. I tried to comfort them the best I could, but how do you comfort someone who's lost a child, especially in such tragic circumstances? It's difficult, that's a skill that I had to unfortunately learn over the course of years, dealing with all sorts of these cases. It's bad, it's rough. See, another thing I learned about suicides is, the people who call us and say they're suicidal aren't the ones who are actually suicidal, they just want attention, they don't actually do it. The people who don't say a word, when there are almost no warning signs, those are the ones who end up dead, and then you have to figure out why. That sticks with you."

I knew it was probably eating him up inside, and I could see the pain on his face. But he continued on, and I let him talk, not saying too much.

"And that's the problem, see, that's what cops have to deal with too. In the long term, all of these family crises that we are exposed to, you know, on a weekly basis, sometimes daily, they stick with us, so every traumatic event which occurs in the community now also becomes my traumatic event. You have your own traumatic events, your own life situations to deal with, but your being sent in the middle all these other crises when the radio goes off, to defend human life, to keep the sanity of your community together, and you just have to do your job. You're wearing fifteen hats, you're a big brother, you're a mediator, you're a priest, you're a shoulder to cry on, you're everything. And you have to go in there every day and solve these problems, so no one gets hurt or killed, and it's a lot of burden to be put on one person."

I had no idea how Charles kept himself together telling me all of this, but he did. That was one of the things I noticed about our interviews which was unbelievable to me. No matter how distressing the memories were, he barely ever needed time to recover from them, and he barely ever showed emotion. During these interviews we would often one or two or three stories in a row that were just unbelievably painful to listen to, and he seemed to be able to get through all of them without any major, outward signs of strife. And true to form, after we finished up that recording on the suicides, he was ready to record again, not even a minute later.

"Yeah, these last two in the DOA category, those are pretty major events in my career by themselves, so let's make sure we get those down," he said, after examining my journal.

"Alright then, let's do it," I said. I hit the start button on the recorder.

"So, for this story, we had made multiple runs at the house of a local couple for, I wouldn't call them domestic violence or domestic disturbances, because he never hit her, probably more like 'verbal altercations.' So, we made runs for verbal altercations between a husband and his wife. They lived in a nice house on one of the nicest streets in the town, a very well-to-do couple in our city. The husband had worked for the federal government agency, and she was highly successful in the private sector in the financial industry. Everything in their life seemed pretty great on the outside, right?"

"But there's always trouble in paradise," I added expectantly.

"Yes, unfortunately there was trouble in their paradise, somewhere in their life there were issues which couldn't be solved between the two of them as a couple, and alcohol stepped in to fill the void. He drank beer, and she drank the heavy stuff, she was partial to gin, and when they'd get drunk she would call us and say he was cheating with some girl, and well, we had dealt with them for so many years that I almost shared parts of their lives with them. So another officer and I, and he was as aware of them as I was, because we had made so many runs to their house, I mean we're talking hundreds or more over a period of years. And one morning we had a run to their house for a DOA."

"I bet that really shook you guys up, just because of how well you knew them."

"It was bad, it was just an awful, awful feeling. We showed up to their house, and as we're going up the concrete steps, up the walkway to their front door, the husband comes out, looking all disheveled, he was obviously heavily intoxicated. I asked him where he was going, I actually called him by his name, and he said, 'Well I'm going to get some more beer,' and then he jerked his thumb backwards towards his house and said, 'Go on in, she's upstairs.'"

"Didn't show any emotion about it, nothing?" I asked.

"No, nothing at all," Charles responded. "That was just the point they were at in their marriage."

Not necessarily a ringing endorsement for lifelong betrothal.

"And he wasn't driving anywhere, right?" I asked.

"No, he wasn't, he just walked about three or four blocks down the street to a gas station, just nonchalant as ever. We knew he wasn't going anywhere, and we were reasonably sure that he hadn't like, murdered her or anything, so we let him go, kind of just shook our heads and went inside, went up the stairs, and opened up the door to the master bedroom. And, I'm telling you man, there was no floor, you couldn't see the floor in their bedroom. It was just all empty gin bottles. The big, gallon plastic ones. And I mean they were everywhere, you could tell that was her nightly thing. She would probably drink one a day."

I raised my eyebrows about as high as they could possibly go. Again, another reality check for me, I hadn't been exposed in my life to any close family member or close friend with an alcohol dependency, much less to that kind of extreme, so the image of their bedroom was a scene I literally had to conjure in my head based on his description.

"Damn," I said. "I really, truly, can't even imagine how it got to that point for them."

"Somehow it did," Charles said. "Somehow, they had gone from you know, local power couple to the local drunks, and she ended up paying the ultimate price. So we're up there, and we're dealing with the things that we have to do. We have to look around and look for any signs of foul play, just our due diligence upon the initial inspection of the scene of a DOA. We look for entrance wounds and exit wounds, and she was naked so that didn't take very long, but it made it all the more difficult. You're thinking about all the times that you dealt with her and the husband, and thinking about all the times you maybe didn't see the signs that things were at the point of no return. Maybe you should have taken the time in your day to talk with them for a little longer, and maybe it wouldn't have gotten so bad. All these thoughts are going through my head, while we're pushing our legs through a sea of gin bottles, and we were there for hours, doing reports, getting outside and inside temperatures, talking to family members, because you also become a grief counselor at that point, if its needed."

"One of the many roles of a police officer."

"That's right. It was just a horrible scene. We literally had to pick her up from the bed and get her out into the hallway, because they couldn't get the gurney cart through all of the bottles. I'm talking hundreds of bottles. And both of us, the other officer and I, it was kind of surreal, we were both talking to each other and saying, 'I remember the last time we talked to her, she was all pissed up and mad at him because he was cheating,' and we were almost reminiscing about those times as good times, you know, because she had been alive."

Charles paused for a moment to collect himself, and I asked Charles the question that had been on my mind the entire time.

"So, what happened to her, you said the husband hadn't done anything to her, right? Did she die of alcohol poisoning or something?"

"Cirrhosis of the liver was what killed her according to the coroner, after several years of alcohol abuse, her body just couldn't handle it anymore. I mean you knew they both had alcohol problems, but you know, seeing it like that was horrible, and then it makes you think about other things. Made me almost blame myself for not doing something sooner."

"Yeah, I wouldn't blame you for thinking that way, anyone would."

After a few seconds of silence, it seemed like he didn't have anything more to say, so I ended the recording.

"Alright, so one more, this last one?" I asked him. "I know you have to head out pretty soon."

Charles nodded.

"Let's get it done, yeah. This one is an important one too, so take some notes while you're listening, just so we make sure to get everything."

I put my hands on my keyboard in readiness.

"Alright, go ahead."

Charles heaved a heavy sigh.

"So, we're towards the end of my career, and I've got everything I've gone through in a twenty-plus year career in my brain, just a lot of stuff that makes it a very pitch black, dark place in my head. And I get a non-responsive infant call, which I'm right around the corner from, put on the lights and sirens and get there in about two minutes. Hoping that it's something that I can help with, you know, maybe I can get a pulse, start CPR, which we're all trained in, just hoping I'll be able to do something. So I pull up, and I'm there before the squad, and as I'm pulling up I recognize the house and the address, it's a place I had gone to several times before, the young lady who lives there has called us multiple times for this thing or that, unrelated incidents. So as I'm walking up, well jogging up to the house, she comes out of the front door carrying a baby, and this child is blue, bluer than my shirt, and she says, "Save my baby, Bell." Uses my name. "Save my baby, Bell." So my focus is obviously on the child, who, for some reason, the mother decides to roll on the grass towards me, she rolls the child about five feet as I'm making my approach on the scene. And I'm looking at this poor little infant, barely three months old, he is the worst color of blue, no pulse, can't really say that rigor mortis has set in, but I can't really tell from the very little information I have about the situation. Was it SIDS, did the baby get crushed somehow or fallen on? So many things could have happened. So I'm holding the child, looking for a pulse, can't find one, so I start infant CPR, and a couple of minutes later the squad comes up, and I get up off the ground and carry the infant over to the ambulance. I'm holding the baby while they continue to try and save him, trying to get a breath, get a pulse, but nothing worked to the point where they had to ask me to let go of the child because they had to take her off toward Children's."

Charles took a deep breath, in and out, putting his hands over his eyes and rubbing them, while looking up to the ceiling. I really didn't have anything to say in response. I thought it would be wise to just let him get everything out.

He continued his monologue.

"Why did another baby have to die, that's the question you have to ask. Why did she have this child if it was only going to die three months later, why did God allow this to happen? After I gave the paramedics the child, it was just, everything came crashing down on me, I went and found a quiet place to just sit and think and fight back screams and tears. You know, another innocent baby has died, they are free of all sin and have done nothing to deserve being taken so early, so why did it happen? And it's now something that I will never forget for the rest of my life, it shows up in my nightmares all the time. "Save my baby, Bell." And then she rolled the baby across the lawn towards me. But I still wonder where God is at when things like this happen, it's a thing that tests your faith, and every bit of strength in side of you, but you just have to get through it and move on to the next run, there's no time for crying or falling apart, you have to respond to the next call."

"You didn't take the day off after that?" I asked.

"No I didn't, had to file my report, and then I went to the hospital to go see what had happened. The baby had died, she was as blue as my shirt and there was not much I could have done, but I tried."

"Yeah, you tried, that's what matters."

"I tried," he repeated.

Chapter Five

"Just another day"

     After getting through a lot of the stories he had to tell which involved death, sadness, and despair, Charles and I decided to focus on some of the more ordinary events from his career, representative of an average day in the life of a city cop. Like we usually did before our weekly interviews, we had discussed over the phone beforehand what topics or stories we thought we should cover, and I would write them down in a list in my journal so him or I wouldn't forget any of them. This would be our longest session to date, with over two hours of recordings, and furthermore, it was an interview I actually enjoyed conducting, and he enjoyed participating in as well. I called to order a pizza and soda just as we were about to get settled and ready to record, and a minute or so later, we began the session.

    "So, we were back on our rotating night shift, and for this story we've had the introduction of the body camera to the force, and it will play a major part."

    "Got it, and what year did this happen?" I asked.

    "It was, um, let me see, it was actually toward the end of my career, early 2016."

    "Cool."

    "So, it's late at night and into a Saturday morning in our city, after a long night of drinking for most, and another officer was dealing with a drunk individual who had refused to pay for his cab, and it was a bit of a slow night actually, so I came over to provide backup. As I parked my car and went over to see what was going on, I see that as the other officer is trying to reason with this guy and talk with him, that the individual in question is attempting to make a phone call, on his credit card, to call his mother for money. He literally took a credit card out of his wallet and was trying to make a call on it, he was so drunk."

"Ha! That's a new one."

"Right? Well it gets even better though. So, while this guy is continuing to try and make a phone on call on his credit card in his drunken state, and he's pushing his finger onto the card like he's dialing numbers, and it's all getting a little ridiculous and I was getting mad. My fellow officer hadn't been able to get him to talk to us, and neither could I."

"So wait, was he just pretending to do it, or did he actually think he was calling his mom?" I asked.

"No, he really did think he was using a cellular device, but it also seemed like he was deliberately ignoring us, too, which is why I was kind of pissed off. So, you know, instead of losing my patience and raising my voice with the guy, I decided that I would go into the store which was right by us and hope that the situation resolved itself with time. So I went past him and went into the gas station, and by this time another officer arrived and they're both out there trying to convince him to talk to them instead of his credit card."

"You were just trying to cool off, weren't you?" I ventured.

"Yeah, I don't know why I became so frustrated with this guy, he was just being belligerent and ignoring us and the whole situation could have been resolved quickly elsewise. Anyway, so I go into the gas station and get a pop, and somewhere along the line I said, 'Hmm, I've got an idea,' and bought another item."

I smiled. "Oh boy."

"So, I walk out there, and he's still on his credit card phone, and now he's complaining that he's not getting any reception, and so I walk up to him, and right now I'm looking at another one of the officers straight into his body camera, he was standing to the left of the guy and I came in from the right, and I said, in full view of the body camera, 'Hey dude, you need to use my phone? It'll get better reception.' And he said, 'Yeah man, thanks.' So I handed him a Kit Kat bar I had just purchased in the store, and so he goes ahead and starts making a phone call on the Kit Kat bar."

"No way."

"And I just turned again and stared directly at the body camera, kind of shook my head a little, and then just walked out of the scene and let them deal with it."

I nodded my approval and shook my head at the same time.

"A Kit-Kat bar cellphone, that's even better. Wow. So, what happened then, the guy ended up getting home I'm assuming?"

"Yeah, so they ended up making a call for him on one of their real phones, and got a hold of one of his roommates who came to get him, and so that was the end of that. After we got off the shift all of us pulled up the footage and were watching it over and over again, laughing our asses off. Good times."

"Sounds like it." I turned off the recording. Another story checked off the list, but we had a lot more to do that day. I referenced my journal again to see what we had on the agenda.

"Next one?" I asked.

"Yeah, let's keep it going, then," he said. "I've got plenty more where that came from."

"How about another funny one?" I asked.

"Yeah, sure, let me see that list really quick."

He inspected the agenda items.

"Actually, you know what, I totally forgot about this one, here's one we've got to put in there." He handed the journal back to me. "Write this down, and type it out in your computer, the story is going to be called 'Kill the puppy.'"

"What?!" I asked. "Kill the puppy? You said it was a funny one, right?"

Charles laughed at how surprised I was.

"Yeah, it's a funny one, trust me!"

I shook my head.

"Alright, if you say so."

I wrote down the title of this new story on our list, and began another recording.

"So, this was another time on our rotating third shift, and like I said, sometimes the nights were long and slow, and it usually started to get dead out around two in the morning. And the other officers were just as bored as you were out on patrol, of course. So, me and another officer, a younger officer who I had trained just recently, we finally get a call and both of us are nearby, so we respond, and it's a loud music complaint in a four family apartment building. And this place was a drug building to be sure, because we had made several drug-related runs to this complex on prior occasions…"

"Does that change the way you approach a call like that, do you go in with more caution if you know you've been there several times before?"

"Well, yes and no, you're always going to a place like this on your guard, but it actually helps us if we've been to a place we've been to before, because we have a good sense of what we're getting into, who's living there, who might be there, what might be there, so there's less unknowns."

I really loved that insight there.

"That's cool, I like that. Sorry, keep going."

"No problem. So we get there, and you have to assume that they're in there doing drugs, but that's not what we're there for, we're there for the loud music complaint. Now if they happen to be stupid enough to open up the door and we see drug paraphernalia or whatever the case might be, then that's a whole new situation."

"Right."

"Well, we knock on the door, and there's no reply. Knock on the door a few more times, still no reply. After about five knocks, you know, the music is still on way too loud, we hadn't even made contact with the people in this apartment yet, so we're running out of options. But then I get this great idea. So, since I speak German pretty well, took German classes all through high school and I was stationed there while I was in the Army, I get the idea to just say the loudest and scariest German phrase I possibly can to scare the living daylights out of these guys enough to get their attention, and so hopefully they would turn down the music."

I cracked a smile. "Here we go."

"So I waited until it sounded like one of their songs was about to end and it was getting a little bit quieter, and I knocked on the door again, and then yelled as loud as I could, 'Die Tur Kummon Ich Macht Die Kliene Hund Betrotten,' which loosely translated means "Come to the door or I'll kill the puppy!" My partner, who is standing on the stairs, asks me what I said, and I told him, and he starts laughing his ass off, just falls to the ground laughing, almost falls down the stairs he's laughing so hard. And then I can hear the guys inside yelling at each other, and one of the said, 'Oh shit, it's the Russians!' And I proceeded to laugh my ass off when I heard that, couldn't have asked for a better reaction, went down exactly like I hoped it would."

"So they turned down the music too, I take it?" I was also laughing my ass off in reaction to the ending, but I just managed to fight through it and ask a somewhat relevant question to keep the dialogue going.

"Yep. After I yelled that and we both almost fell down the stairs from laughing so hard, we heard all of them run to the back of the apartment like a herd of elephants, and the music subsequently gets shut down, so that was mission accomplished. And the rest of the night the other officers were sending me videos of themselves saying all kinds of bullshit German-sounding phrases and asking me 'What did I say, what did I say?' And I'm like 'Nothing, you didn't say shit.' It was a great night."

"Sounds like it."

"Alright so another day in the life of a police officer. We had a crime in progress going on at a local sunglasses store, they had some people who had broken into the shop and they were stealing some of their expensive sunglasses, like the Dolce and Gabbana sunglasses and Ray-Bans and all the nicer brands. And this was this group's second hit too, we figured out later that they had also robbed a store in northern Kentucky. So when the robbery began, one of the employees immediately hit the silent alarm, but these guys were good, they were quick, and they come in and steal upwards of ten thousand dollars-worth of these really expensive sunglasses, and so it was in and out, and they're in their car and it was off to the races."

"Sounds like they had a good plan, yeah."

"But we were on to them, though, somebody saw the car they got into and so we were tracking them, we had information coming in about their location as they're fleeing minute by minute, and so we're flying over to where they are full speed. And it just so happens as I'm going toward the outdoor shopping center where the store was located, I'm about four streets down, the car passes me in the opposite direction."

"Nice!"

"So I put on my lights so I can turn around, do a big U-turn, get behind them and then right as I'm just about to catch up, he decides to take it to the highway, because right near there is the entrance ramp, he could have turned right or left but he decided to kick the pursuit up to a high speed chase. And so he's weaving in and out of traffic, slow lane, fast lane, middle lane, and I'm right on his tail, trying not to hit everybody in the process, you have to concentrate on what you're doing until another officer arrives to call the pursuit, because at that point I'm engaged in the pursuit and calling the pursuit as it happens, and also trying to figure out whether I should abandon the pursuit because it's getting too dangerous."

"Didn't even know that was an option, to suspend a chase like that," I commented.

"Well the safety of the public is paramount, especially in these high-speed chases, so if the situation is getting too risky then you just have to find another way to catch up to him, you know, you give the vehicle description to the state troopers or to the officers in the next jurisdiction over, or try to continue to track them by helicopter if that's an option. So, finally another car joins up behind me, and he starts calling pursuit, and I'm still on the guy, right behind him. The traffic is workday traffic near the end of the day, after rush hour but still a pretty significant number of cars, so once we kind of get into a heavier flow section of the highway, the only place he can go to gun it really fast is the shoulder."

"Well that probably wasn't smart."

"It was definitely dangerous, he was out of the way of the cars for the most part because everybody was moving over for us, but it was still pretty tight quarters to navigate, with traffic on our left and the guardrails on our right, doing over a hundred miles per hour. Talk about sweating bullets, man, because the guardrail is just inches from your rearview mirror, but I'm not even thinking about how crazy the situation is, it's all instinct really. I'm just focusing on what he's doing and trying to stay in pursuit relatively safely. So after about two minutes I'd say, we finally get to a part where the guardrail stops, and there's an open field there, and the car literally just slides into the field, and they put on the brakes and everybody hops out and starts running, there's two of them. The other police car heads to the next exit and goes up the road to try and head them off, my car is in the field, and I'm now in foot pursuit. They break off from each other, and one of them heads toward where the other officer was headed, so I let him go and get after the other guy."

"So now it's part two of the chase," I added.

"Yep, time to get the running shoes on. So the suspect crosses the field with me hot on his trail, and we get into some woods which lead to the backyard of some houses. Once we get into the woods, I entered, but since he had had about a fifteen second head start, so I slow down a bit, because I don't know where he is at that point.

He could be waiting to ambush me or he could have kept on running, I had no way of knowing. So I'm being careful, got my gun out, just waiting for him to jump out from behind a tree or a bush or something and attack me, and thankfully he doesn't. Once I get through the woods, I have to cut through some heavy bushes and into an open backyard, and here's where it gets interesting."

"Okay."

He continues. "I'm in this backyard and right in front of me is the back porch on the property, and there's an old man sitting there with some food on the grill. Stooped up right next to him was who I believed to be the suspect. He was out of breath, taking heavy breaths, but he was just sitting down in one of the chairs next to the old man. The old guy, he was probably seventy years old, he's not saying a word, just chilling there, and I'm telling the young guy, the suspect, 'Get on the ground man, get on the ground!' And then he says to me, 'What we're barbequing man, we're barbequing at my grandpa's house, what do you want?' When he said that, I definitely had a moment, I was tired and, you know, mentally and physically stressed from the chase, and so my brain had to sit and process what he was saying for a second, and then I got back to my senses and I'm thinking to myself, 'No, that's not right,' so I tell him again, I said 'That's bullshit, get on the ground!' He still doesn't budge from the chair though."

"What did he think was going to happen, that you were going to run by and ask if they had seen someone running, and they would say, 'He went that way!' like in the movies?"

"Who knows, but I'm not that dumb, that's for sure. And yeah, so here's the kicker, so just for good measure I look over to the old man and I say "Sir, do you know him?" And this guy, without even missing a beat, said "Nope." And I guess he had some chewing tobacco in his mouth, because right after he said that, he spit it out almost for the effect or something. It was the funniest thing, just without missing a beat this old guy responds to me and spits out his chew, I had to laugh about it later. But then of course, the kid knew the jig was up, and so he got up from his chair and tried to hop over the side of the porch and run again, but I got over there and tackled him in the middle of the side yard."

"Nice job!" I exclaimed. "So what about the other guy?"

"Well the other cop was still driving around trying to locate the other guy, and I think they got him. So I take my guy on the walk of shame in cuffs, about ¾ of a mile through the woods and across the field back to my car, and the whole time he's fighting and pulling and I'm yelling at him, I'm cussing him out, saying '110 on the highway, what the fuck, are you crazy?' and 'A barbeque man, what the fuck do you think I am, stupid?' So we get to my car and we both get a chance to calm down, because now I've got to clear my head and get all the details down for the paperwork after I take him to jail."

"What kind of paperwork?" I asked.

"Well I had to do my regular report, and then a pursuit report, and on the pursuit report I had to articulate why I was doing 110 miles per hour down the shoulder of an interstate, and it took me late into the night to finish all of that, so you know. That was just another day."

"So, we made a run for a possible wanted subject in a house, it was a family, of course, that we were familiar with, they lived in the third story of a multi-family house. We quietly work our way up the stairs on the side of the house, trying not to sound like a herd of buffalo, get to the door, and the guy's son answers it. As we're talking to him, explaining why we're there, we hear shuffling inside, in the back of the house, and so naturally we asked him about it. We said 'Hey, is your dad here,' and he says, 'No, no, I'm here by myself,' but you could still hear movement inside, and the son had the door open just enough that you could see the dad flying past the living room and into the next room. So at that point we were justified in entering the residence, we had observed a wanted suspect in the residence, so we pushed through the door past the son and went in to apprehend the father."

"I really should educate myself more on those laws, you know, about when police can legally enter a residence and when they can't," I quipped. "Not that I'm going around committing crimes, but just for the sake wanting to be a more informed citizen. Does it vary from state to state?"

"The laws can be different from state to state, yes, but generally police are allowed to enter a residence without a warrant when there's exigent circumstances. So in this case, we're literally chasing him through the house, going from room to room, and it was kind of funny really. But then for some reason, when he gets to the back room and he knows he's cornered, he feels that this warrant is so bad, so terrible, that he needed to jump out the third story window to get away from us."

"No way, seriously?"

"Yeah I know, he was desperate. He thought he was going to go through the window, jump out, hit the grass and get away. But that's not what happens, of course. When he climbs through the window and jumps down, he ends up crashing into this bass boat, an old metal fishing boat, that was parked in the back of the driveway, lands on the motor actually, and when we get down there he's bleeding and in horrible pain basically, he had broken a few bones, that's for sure."

"All that over what kind of warrant, what was it for?" I asked.

"So his warrant was for missing child support payments, so it wasn't even anything that incredibly serious from a law enforcement standpoint. Why he decided to jump out a third story window over it, I don't know. If he had just taken the time to talk to us, we would have taken him down to the station, worked with him and tried to figure out what the deal was, see what was going on in his life that was causing him to miss the child support payments, and maybe try to help him. You know, he would have done a little time in jail regardless, but maybe he could have bonded out, you know. He didn't have to go running and hurt himself."

"So would that be kind of a message that you would want the general public to understand about interactions with police over warrants? Just to say, you know, that there can be a peaceful resolution, there doesn't have to be conflict?"

"Like I said, I honestly just wish people would talk to us. If you know you've got a warrant and you've done something you shouldn't have, it's not necessarily the end of the world, right, it doesn't have to be the end of the rope. We're trying to help you, not hurt you. Instead of giving in to that fight or flight instinct, just don't escalate the situation needlessly. Rational communication and dialogue are what separates us from the animals. Unless you've raped or murdered somebody, or killed an officer, you know, if you're a perpetrator of those types of crimes, then we'll probably bring the pain and come after you if that's the case. But if it's something that you have a good chance to recover from and re-enter society at some point after you've served your time, you should work with us, not against us. Might make the difference between becoming a repeat offender and not. So that's all I have to say about that, yeah. My job is already hard enough, you know, I don't want to hurt you, you don't want to hurt me, you don't want to get yourself hurt. Serving warrants, officers are going to be as respectful as possible, but we will match what you give us. So if you're respectful, we'll be respectful. But it doesn't go that way most of the time unfortunately. We're providing a service to the public, we are public servants, and at the end of the day, it's also a job, we're just working a job and we don't want to get hurt while we're doing our job. So wait until you hear what officers have to say before you fight, and just stop, think and listen."

"For this story, I'll just begin by saying that life sends all of us serious loops, people's lives can change in an instant and without warning, or sometimes the change is slow and creeping but then it hits you, and suddenly, you don't know how to react. I made a run to a home that had been foreclosed on, gas and electric was shut off, no water, and the gentleman refused to leave the home. He didn't feel it was fair, didn't feel it was right, and mostly just couldn't handle the loss of his house. So, we responded because we had gotten tipped off by a family member that he was in the house with a gun and barricaded himself into a back room, and so several of us officers showed up to see if we could resolve the situation."

"It really just blows my mind, the variety of circumstances you guys have to deal with, it's a lot more than you might think of at first," I said.

Charles nodded. "We have to be there for all kinds of personal crises and the times when the circumstances of life are just too much to handle. You see a lot. So, back to the story, after searching the house, we located the man down a hallway and in one of the small bedrooms in the house, and so we set up a perimeter at the entrance to the hallway, and we had a guy outside with a rifle and a scope so we could see what was going on inside the room through the window. I was the one with the shield, so I was in front and talking to the guy. Had my duty weapon drawn, knelt down behind my shield, and tried to start a dialogue with him."

"So what do you say at first, how do you even start that conversation?" I asked.

"Well, you address him by his name if you have it, and if you don't have it, then you ask for it. Well actually, even if you do have his name you still ask him what his name is, and you tell him yours. Establishes a bit of a personal connection between the two of you. This situation was different though, unfortunately, because the guy just refused to talk with us."

"Oh wow, really?"

"Yeah, and it went on for hours, I was yelling out to him for about the first five minutes, asking him questions, you know, trying to even get him to say something, but he didn't. After a few minutes went by, he stuck his head out to look at us, to look at where we were, but then he stuck his head back inside and closed the door. And this would happen every fifteen minutes probably, I would say a few words to him, and he would stick his head out, and I every time he did I would tense up thinking it was time for the shootout, you know, I would say to myself every time he opened the door, 'this is it, I don't want do this,' and then he'd put his head back in and we'd start all over again. For about three hours we were talking to him, I tried to reason with him, but he never talked back, he never said anything, not once. We thought of everything we could to tell him to get him to come out peacefully, to impress upon him that everything was going to be okay. His life wasn't worth the house, he would get a new one eventually, life would go on, it would get better. But nothing got through to him, no matter how much I begged and pleaded with him."

"Can't imagine why," I wondered.

"Like I said man, we see people at their most desperate times. This guy was just too far gone mentally, he had checked out from life entirely. So eventually SWAT came in, and they replaced us on the scene, and when negotiations failed with them, they decided to end the standoff, so they flash-banged the hallway and tried to get him out, but the situation ended up in a shooting unfortunately, an officer-related shooting."

"So he probably wanted a suicide by cop, it seems like," I said.

"That was probably the case, yes. These types of situations, when it comes to those hardships in life, when you can't pay the bills or you find yourself hungry or out on the street, this is another case when someone lost their life because of those hardships. So, as police officers, we want people to know that without difficulties in life, you're not going to get better. Police officers have the same problems as regular folks, we're no different from you, and we see people at their lowest points every day. The old adage of course is that what doesn't kill you makes you stronger, but in this case, it did kill him, and it was just really a sad situation. Unfortunately, this event in his life killed him. And you know, as a result of me being exposed to all these situations, people being at the lowest points in their lives, I just want people to know that you can get through it, and things can get better, and don't give up. Ultimately, the police are here to help and not hurt you."

"That's a good message."

"So, let's go all the way back to when I was being trained as an officer, a new officer on the force. I was fresh off of riding with my field training officer, and in those days, it wasn't this long program that we eventually developed it into, back then it was about two weeks riding in the car with my trainer, and then it was like, 'Okay he's ready, get him out there.' So I was out on my own."

"And what year was this again?"

"This was 1999. So, it had been less than a week after the field training, my first week out being in my own car, and I'm working the second shift. There's a little store, kind of a mom and pop store that's in the middle of a residential area, and a call comes in that there was an armed robbery in progress with a subject with a bandana wrapped around his face, firearm in his hand. So I'm close by, so I cut down through a back street that's behind where the shops are and then come to a light that's about two blocks away from the store, and I was still far enough away that I couldn't cut my sirens yet, so I had my sirens on and I'm going code, got lights flashing and sirens blaring."

"Oh, so do you usually cut your sirens at a certain point before approaching a potential crime scene?"

"Yeah, so we cut the sirens off at a certain point, because that noise carries pretty far. I'd say six to eight blocks out would be when I would kill my sirens. So, I'm at this light, there's a red light, and I go around and to the left of the car that's stopped at the red light, and then stop at the intersection and change my tones, to the high-low, wee-woppers, and I look to make sure that no one is coming through too fast and everybody sees me coming. I see a car coming, and, that's the reason why you change tones at lights is so the people coming through know that something is coming. Sometimes a police siren might just be regular background noise to some folks, but if you hear a different tone that forces you to be aware and look around to find the source of the noise. So I make eye contact with this car that's approaching the intersection, and I see the front end of her car dip down as she's braking, and so I assume that she sees me and that she's going to brake like she's supposed to and let me go through."

"Uh oh."

"Yeah, you already know how this story ends. So, I see her braking and pull on through the intersection. Well unfortunately, she gets nervous for some reason and decides to floor it right after she put on her brakes, right as I'm going through the intersection! And so she guns it and runs straight into the side of my car, pushes me across the intersection and slams me into a telephone pole. Thankfully I wasn't injured too bad, my car was obviously not in good shape, her car, the front end of her car was on top of mine, and I basically had to climb out of the passenger side window to extricate myself from the cruiser."

"What the hell, though?" I asked. That was all I could really say in response. "Why did she go through?"

"We'll get to that. So, once I finally got myself out, I went around to go check on her, she was fine but a little shaken up. And once I got her out of her car, I asked her what was going on, and she said she hadn't heard my sirens, and that that intersection in particular always made her nervous. I guess she panicked, she was trying to get through the intersection, and maybe she saw me but didn't know I was trying to get through, whatever it was. So that was a great first week, the guy who was my field training officer happened to also be on the shift with me and was also responding to the robbery, and so he comes through the same intersection from the direction the lady had come from, he radios to see if I'm okay, but then he just flies by me towards the scene and proceeds to laugh his ass off at my expense over the radio."

"'Nice job, rookie!'" I said, imitating what his field training officer might have said.

"Yeah, right? Well so he gets down there and it ends up being a teenager with a pellet gun, he gets there in the nick of time to make an arrest, kid didn't get hurt, so that night ended smoothly, but my night didn't of course. I had to go to the hospital, get myself checked out, get medically cleared for duty."

"Did you have to fill out any paperwork or anything about the incident?"

"For sure, I mean, we had to have an accident investigator come out and officially determine and verify what happened on the scene. They ended up interviewing the person who was stopped at the light, the person who was in the car that I had to go around when I stopped at the intersection to make sure it was safe to go through, and she was saying 'Yeah he stopped and changed his tone, and I was sitting there in disbelief watching the other person charge through the intersection and take out the cop car.' So, I mean, the lady who hit me ended up being at fault for the accident, but here's the kicker, here's the crazy part. So obviously that was a pretty bad accident, right, and even though I'm in a city vehicle, even though I'm on the job, guess what? That accident ends up on my driving record, and my insurance goes up, even though I'm being covered by the city."

"Seriously? That doesn't seem fair."

"No, it's not."

I pressed the stop button to cut us off there, but soon after, we decided to push through and record another, related anecdote before we took another break.

I started us off.

"Yeah, so I remember you saying that you went through some specialized training during your career, and accident investigation was one of them?" I asked.

"That's right. I went to several schools for automobile accident training, went to the FBI, went to crime scene photography courses, got certified in that, so I ended up not only taking pictures for the Major Accident Team, but I ended up taking pictures for almost every crime scene I went to, just because I was certified and available, so it was easier to have me do it. And so for this story, this has to do with a violent purse snatcher who had been hitting our two major shopping centers, and other shopping centers around the city, and he was attacking elderly ladies quite aggressively, knocking them to the ground and stuff, so it was a multi-jurisdictional deal, and he was boosting cars too, grand theft auto."

"Real quality individual," I quipped.

"Real stand-up guy, right. So, we had a call come in from an officer who was off duty and in plainclothes who recognized him while he was out at one of our shopping centers, and the suspect was there and seemed to be scoping people out, and so when we got the call from dispatch we moved in on him to see what was going on, and he saw us and bolted, and a pursuit followed. The pursuit was going on, he had gotten into his vehicle, it was his personal vehicle, not a car he had stolen, but it went through our city into another city, and so they added one of their cars to our pursuit. And so what happened was he got to an intersection, and a lady started to turn left, and the purse snatcher just slammed straight into her car, just straight t-boned her, killed her instantly."

"Damn, that's terrible."

"Needless loss of life, exactly, just hurts your soul, man. So from an accident investigation perspective, we have to show what he did, show the recklessness of his act, there was obviously no intent on his part to kill the lady, but of course that was what ended up happening, and so he ended up getting charged with negligent vehicular homicide. On top of multiple counts of theft and assault. So as the crime scene photographer, I had to do three hundred and sixty degree photos around the whole car, photos walking in the direction the car that was hit had been traveling, in the direction the purse snatcher's vehicle had been travelling, photos of all the minute details of the damage, what direction the debris travelled, so you know exactly where the cars were headed, final resting position, impact position, and then to get a better vantage point of the whole scene, I went up to the top floor of an office building that was right by the intersection and shot some photos from up above on top of the roof."

"That's pretty cool."

"It was actually, I had another officer hold me over the edge of the building a bit while I was trying to get a good angle and get a panoramic view, so we got a kick out of that. So, due to our whole reconstruction effort we ended up getting the conviction, and the damage tells the whole story of course, you can ask eyewitnesses what happened but ultimately the damage on the scene will give you the clearest picture. Where the car was hit, the speed at the point of impact, you could tell who was at fault, the lady had been turning left at a normal speed on a green arrow, and the purse snatcher hadn't been trying to evade or anything, so even though there wasn't traffic cam footage, we knew that he had just flown through the intersection on a red light and completely blindsided this lady and killed her, so we were able to get a conviction, eighteen years in prison. And I got a letter from the chief of the nearby city where the accident had occurred that, you know, it was my hard work that helped us get him convicted and take him off the streets."

"Nice, great job!"

"Thanks. We had a lot of responsibilities on Major Accident Team, it's not for simple accidents or fender-benders, it was for bad ones where there was normally a fatality involved. Not only did you do the picture taking and accident reconstruction, but you also got to use some awesome tools, there was a lot of science and math involved. Mostly what you're doing is bringing out this thing called a TOTAL station, and it's a really neat tool that's used by land surveyors usually, but it can also help you fix the point of impact on the street and the position of the cars in an accident situation, a very valuable tool. We had one time where there was a truck that was too high to go under an overpass, and the truck stopped immediately and the car behind it couldn't stop, and just destroyed everybody inside, and we had to use the TOTAL station to figure out exactly what happened and corroborate the driver's testimony. That accident was pretty bad, I mean that car, there was nothing left of it, or the people inside of it. There was another time, I got called out to a scene at three in the morning for an accident on the highway involving a drunk driver, we had one guy that was going so fast and was so drunk that he slid sideways when he was trying to change lanes, hit a metal light post, which cut the car in half, and the guy rode the front part of the car into a bridge embankment and all the way up to the top, and walked away. Thankfully he didn't hurt anybody, but when we got to court with him he was trying to give us some bullshit excuses, trying to get out of paying for some of the fines and damages."

"That's ridiculous, what the hell?" I exclaimed.

"Yeah so you get people like that. But there are times that are just heartbreaking too, we had a girl who had hit a guardrail post, and she was a young, inexperienced driver, she had lost control of her car and went into a spin, hit right at the end of the guardrail where there's a big, square, metal plate with bolts in it, and it punched right through the driver's side door and killed her instantly. You have to contact the parents, comfort them on the scene of such a tragedy. And in situations like this, where the fault lies in the fatality, and that's a terrible thing, but you have to keep it real. There are times when you can immediately tell where the fault lied for a particular accident, if it was excessive speed or recklessness on the part of the driver, or if it was environmental or road conditions, or if there were other externalities. The girl, the roads were a little slick because it had just rained heavily, maybe she was going a bit too fast and wasn't meaning to, and just wasn't experienced enough as a driver to know how to drive safely in those conditions, and those are the kind of situations that just break your heart."

I shook my head.

"Yeah, what do you even say to the parents in that situation? So much grief already."

"It's tough man, it's not an easy thing for the officer on scene. But some of them were like heart attacks, driving straight into the woods, overdose, drive straight into a guardrail post, there were just hundreds, and just adds to the death that you see over your career as a police officer."

On that note, we took our second break of the session, so Charles went out to smoke, and I didn't really have much to do myself, except to maybe eat the rest of our pizza. Usually we would split the pizza we ordered evenly, but sometimes he would let me have more than my share, partly because I was a college student and it was a staple of my diet, but also because it was often difficult for Charles to eat foods like pizza because of his surgeries. It was something I had noticed during our early interviews, that he would sometimes seem to have trouble swallowing food, and it confused me for a few weeks, but then, once he told me about all of the operations he had undergone around his neck and throat area, it made more sense.

We only had one or two stories left on the agenda to cover that day, but thankfully they were easy ones, no painful memories involved.

"So this one is about a time when you were on television, right?" I asked.

"Yep, this story is for all the people who love to watch COPS and Live P.D., all those shows, we had them ride along with us for a few days, and so I'll tell you what happened with all that."

"Sweet."

"So, we had the COPS crew in our car, and we were supposed to be responding to a possible drug deal gone bad, involving a guy with a knife. Well, myself and another officer were at the door of the address we were called to, and had another two-man car parked next to the vehicle which had been described to us by the dispatch, and we could hear these guys moving inside as we were banging on the door, and the suspect goes out the back door and loops around to get to his car, but there he meets up with the other officers, and an altercation occurs down there, and COPS is right there filming it all."

"Live action all the way," I said.

"It's live action, they get everything on camera. So, the guy runs towards the car to try and hop in and drive away, but he gets tased as he is sitting in the driver's seat trying to start his car. Somehow, he got his muscles to agree with him and he was able to start the car and drive off, cutting the wires from the taser and taking everything with him. We pursued him through several jurisdictions, ended up pursuing him into a community center, you know with a swimming pool and basketball hoops and stuff for kids?"

"Yeah."

"And my moment of glory was my Dukes of Hazard slide across the hood of my car, and tackling and taking the suspect into custody, I was the third man in the pursuit but I happened to get to him first. So then we had to get him to the hospital because he was a bit shaken up, had some injuries, and when we get there, he was trying to make all kinds of deals with the COPS crew in exchange for signing the consent to let them air the footage, he wanted them to bring him a steak dinner, bring him a carton of cigarettes, and he finally decided to give consent, which ended up being titled 'Tased and Confused' and got aired on one of the shows," Charles concluded.

"That's cool. I personally never watched COPS, I don't know why, I think my parents probably thought it was too violent or something. Or at least, they wanted me to grow up seeing the police as my friends."

"Well they were good parents then, because that stuff is definitely not for children."

"Yeah, I guess not."

We didn't stop for very long before recording the last story of the day. Charles had just picked up a new job about half an hour outside the city limits, and his shift was two o'clock to ten, so we would usually finish up around one and then he would drive up to work. We had about fifteen minutes before he had to go.

"Ready for this last one, the traffic stop story?" I asked.

"Yeah, I'm good."

I paused to make sure my recorder was ready.

"Alright, and go."

"Okay, so one more funny story from the daily patrols, I think this will be a good addition. So, we had what was called 'traffic detail,' and it was basically us going out to try and catch speeders in our jurisdiction, and this meant we would go out on our section of the highway and post up in certain spots, and you could either run radar or laser when you're posted up. I usually tended to run radar because there was really no place to park sideways in our jurisdiction. So, I had a vehicle that went by me around ninety miles per hour, pulled out and tracked the car down, and initiated the traffic stop. I could see the car had a personal plate, which I can't give you the details of obviously, but I'll just say it said something along the lines of God or Jesus, a religious theme basically. So, I pulled her over, and you approach the car on the right-hand side to stay out of the way of traffic, and when I got up there, as soon as I knocked on the window and rolled it down, the lady immediately starts saying out loud "Lord Jesus help me!" And that caught me off guard, that threw me for a loop for a second."

"Yeah, I'd be surprised too," I said.

"But here's the great part, so after the second time she says 'Lord Jesus help me,' she follows it up with, "Lord Jesus, please don't let..." and then she physically paused and read my nameplate, "Officer Bell give me a ticket, please Lord, help him do the right thing!" and then she repeated the same thing immediately, just went right on going again, looking to me and then up to the sky saying, "Lord, please help Officer Bell do the right thing, please Lord!" And I honestly couldn't handle it, I was laughing so hard, I just couldn't take it, and after I recovered I was just like, "Go ahead and go on your way, M'am, just watch how fast you're going, alright?" After a performance like that, I just couldn't bring myself to write her one. The story was worth it in my mind. And then as I was walking away and she was rolling up the window, she wasn't thanking me, she was still talking to God, she was saying, "Thank you Lord Jesus for not making Officer Bell write me a ticket!" I just couldn't deal with it, the performance was too great, because she literally paused mid-sentence to look at my name tag and insert my name into her prayer, like she had done it a hundred times before. Anyway, so that was a traffic stop story, score one for Jesus on that one."

"I guess, that's crazy." I shook my head. "I don't think that's how prayer is supposed to work, but you know, to each their own."

"Right."

We ended the session on that note, with Jesus interceding at a traffic stop, and Charles got up and went outside to smoke before he left for work. I was sure that there were hundreds and hundreds more stories from his career that he was leaving out, either because they were too mundane, or too depraved, but in my mind, it didn't matter that we couldn't record everything. What was more important were the messages behind the stories, and the lessons that those stories could teach everyday Americans about the darker side of the society in which they lived. Everyone has a different reality they face in their daily lives, and everyone is shaped by that reality. Their thoughts, opinions, and beliefs are shaped by what they see, or at the very least, by what they tell themselves that they are seeing. For me, it was a privilege to experience the life of a city cop through Charles' anecdotes, given that, if I had never met him, that was not likely to be a perspective which I might ever have the chance to gain during the course of my own life.

Chapter Six

"Disheartening"

      Although the label had been applied to him several times during his career, and his achievements certainly proved it, you would never catch Charles calling himself a hero. He would always tell me that he was just trying his best to help people, and that he strived to deliver a consistent effort in service to the community whenever his name was called. His actions in the story that follows garnered him official recognition for his heroism, and commendations from fellow officers nationwide, but true to his personality, he would say it was all simply done in the line of duty, just another part of the sometimes-thankless job of being a police officer in the United States of America.

      "So, I was working overnights 11-7 in the morning, we were rotating shifts, or I might even have been on permanent third shift at this point, I can't remember exactly, but, it was probably nearer to the beginning of the shift at around 1 o'clock in the morning, and we get a run to one of the dead-end streets in the town for a fight, with a gun, at least, that's what we were told by dispatch. We, my partner and I, responded code, got down there, and we were prepared, getting out of the car with guns drawn, but here was the thing. As we were getting closer to the address, you could see that there was smoke billowing into the sky, and that confused us for a minute."

      "Yeah, I was just about to ask you about that," I put in. "You guys were probably driving up to the place, and then you see smoke and fire but no fire trucks. I'm betting that was the first sign that something was wrong."

This was one of the first stories Charles had told me about his career when he and I first got to know each other, and so I already had a good idea of what was going to happen as he was speaking. However, I still decided to ask questions throughout the conversation, perhaps to help jog his memory about details he may have forgotten.

"That's exactly right, it took us about a minute once we arrived at the scene to get out of our cars and figure out what was really going on. The neighbors were yelling to us that it was a fire, and they were saying 'there are babies in there, babies are in there, you have to do something!'"

There was one detail that I wasn't sure about, though.

"Wait, so why didn't they send the fire department again?" I asked. "I can't remember if you told me about that or not."

Charles nodded in response to my question. "It was actually due to a language barrier issue. See, what had happened was that a Hispanic guy had called it in, and they thought he had said there was a 'fight broken out with a gun,' but what he actually said was that there was a 'fire and the mother is gone.' So obviously once we see the smoke and flames, I called into dispatch immediately and let them know that it was a fire, not a fight, so they could call the fire department, and my partner and I approached the apartment complex."

"So the mom was gone, and the kids caused a fire somehow?"

"Yeah, that's exactly what happened. The mom was a drug addict who was known to us in the neighborhood, and she had basically gone out to smoke crack. She had no electricity in the apartment, possibly no water, and what had happened was that she always had candles behind the couch to, you know, provide the home with some light, and she had left another person, who was also a crack addict, to watch the babies while she was out. But the problem was, that that guy also left to go and smoke crack too, and the candles got knocked over by one of the kids. So the couch went up in flames, and then the walls and ceiling, and next thing you know, the kitchen and the whole rest of the place from there, filling up with black smoke quicker than you could possibly imagine."

"Wow. Well, so you guys have to act in that situation, right?"

"There really wasn't a choice in our minds, my partner and I, we knew we had to do something, because every second the fire rescue was taking to get there was just an increased chance that the kids would die from smoke inhalation. So, we kicked down the door and I went in first, got a little flash of heat and light, and the smoke was heavy, as thick as could be, couldn't see two inches in front of my face. So I came back out, regrouped, got some air, and him and I at that point just said, 'Fuck it, if we die we die, let's go' and we charge inside. Well we didn't charge of course, we cautiously made our way inside as quickly as possible, because literally all you could see was pretty much the glow of the fire on the ceiling through the smoke, and that was it. You could feel pieces of ceiling falling on you and burning the top of your head, your clothes."

"So essentially there was zero visibility, couldn't see the walls or anything?"

"Pretty much, and our eyes were either closed or squinting the entire time, putting our hands in front of us and to the left and right to make sure we didn't run into anything, and taking careful steps. We negotiated our way to the back of the apartment and we could hear the coughing, because the kids were certainly about to be overcome by smoke inhalation. There was so much smoke, just so much smoke…"

Charles sighed, and his voice trailed off. The pain in his eyes was unmistakable as he recalled the scene. After a few seconds, he continued with the story.

"So, we got back there, feeling our way, and I felt the head of a child, so I grabbed one, and my partner did the same, he grabbed another one, and we worked our way out again through the smoke, with the children against our chests. And now the flames are getting even more extreme in the living room, and so we covered the kids tighter with our torsos and arms to protect them, and just busted through the fire and got outside. In my arms was a little girl, around four years old, and I put my coat around her and then headed back in for the last child, there was one more. And as I was doing that, the fire trucks finally showed up, because they hadn't been dispatched when they needed to be dispatched because of the misinterpretation over the 911 call, obviously we hadn't known it was a fire, and everything had happened so quickly. I was about to negotiate my way back to the third child when they all came in with their equipment and told me to get out, so they could handle the rest of the situation, so they got the third child out very soon after, and then put the fire out."

I took a deep breath. As I said, I had already known what the ending of the story would be, but it didn't make it any less intense as I was listening to him tell it.

"Thank God, holy shit. That's just insane, just insane."

"It was insane, it was a very frightening and very terrible situation. So as they were putting out the fire, my partner and I were in the ambulance with the two kids we had just saved and the paramedics, and we all went down to UC Medical, where I was just blowing black shit out of my nose, coughing it up, spitting out just pure, black charcoal, and I ended up having permanent damage to the functioning of my lungs because of that, and I still got some white scarring on the top of my head here where the little bits of ceiling were coming down on top of me, see?"

He lowered his head and pointed.

"Oh my God, there it is, yeah, that looks like it hurt."

"Well that was the least of my concerns at the time. I had to go on an oxygen tank for a bit to try and get the smoke out of my lungs, and so did my partner, he had to do that too. And then the next day, the press shows up to talk to us, and him and I went down to the apartment complex because they wanted us to do interviews there, and show footage of the building and how damaged it was, I guess to show what we had walked through to rescue the kids."

I nodded. "So, can you recreate the scene in more detail then, describe what it looked like after the fire?"

"Yeah, of course, I'll walk you through the scene. So, I mean, there was barely anything left obviously, just a shell of an apartment, whole thing was black charcoal, looked like a log that had just gotten done burning in a fireplace. The couch was almost completely gone except for a few pieces of debris, and all you could see to know that there had been a couch there was an imprint of the legs that had been etched into the floor by the fire. The apartment lay out was like this, you got a front door, straight into the living room, kitchen is off to the right, a little hallway to the left, with two bedrooms on the right and left sides of the hallway and a bathroom in the back. The fire was in the living room, and it was on the second floor, so there was no way to reach the kids from outside or from a window, so our only option had been to go through the fire. The fire department, they were mad as hell at us, because we took live ammo in there in our guns, but you know, we were trying to save kids, we weren't really thinking about that in the moment."

"Yeah, I didn't even think about that, either, the ammunition. That could have been bad if the ammo had cooked off," I added.

"There were a lot of things we didn't think about, but like I said, we were just trying to save these kids, and that was our main objective. So, back to the scene, so we were there with the press answering questions, and it really didn't hit me until I saw that burned up, shell of an apartment, I was like, 'Fuck, I went through that?' And they asked me, 'Well, why did you do it, why did you go through the fire to save these kids?' and I mean, I was surprised by the question, and I'll say it again, so I told them, 'Well there were kids in the building and we were responding so we had to do something.' I mean, it's not much more complicated than that. If it were my kids, I would sure as hell want the first responder to do something, whether it was a fire fighter or a cop or whoever. So yeah, just really no choice but to act decisively in that situation."

"Well, I commend you, my friend, that was a brave thing you did."

"I appreciate it, man. I got enough praise for it though, probably a little too much to be honest. My partner and I, we received police medals of valor for our actions, the life-saving medal, we got a letter from

Congress, plaques from the VFW, all kinds of people made a big deal out of it, and even when we went to court the judges would stop proceedings and make everybody clap for us when we walked in the courtroom. But here was kind of the sad part, well I won't call it sad, more like umm, what's the word?"

"Disheartening?"

Unfortunately, I knew exactly which word he was looking for.

"Yes, disheartening, and disappointing. So, a year had passed after the fire, and I end up going back to that same apartment building on a random call, a loud music complaint. And what happened was, the landlord had apparently rebuilt that apartment and put the mother and kids back in there again. So, like I said, loud music complaint, it was during the day, I guess an older lady had called it in because some kids had their stereo turned up loud and she was trying to take her afternoon nap, and so I went by the address and took care of it. After that, as I was walking out to my car, and the same family was coming out of their new apartment, and the little girl who I had saved, she recognized me and was running up to come say hi to me. You know, just being a little kid. She was so precious. But the mother, who I guess was pissed off because she had gotten charged with child endangerment because of the incident and had had to pay a fine, she says to her little girl "Get away from the police, they're racist and evil and they don't care about you." And you know, that just absolutely killed me right there, that was like a knife to the heart. I was disappointed, to say the least."

I shook my head.

"I wouldn't blame you one bit."

"I was just flabbergasted. How can you raise a child of five years old who was saved by the police and teach them that the police are evil? All in all, we're just like everybody else. It doesn't change anything, we're all human, there's no difference. Because of course, the big story out of this situation was, after the story got out in the news and people, you know, saw that I and my partner were white and the kids were black, people recognized that even though there was a difference in race between us and the victims of the fire, that's not a thought that even remotely runs through our minds in that moment, our mission was to go get the children out of the fire, that's it, no different than what a fire fighter or fire rescue does. So, it just hurt me inside to have the mother say that, and she came up and grabbed the little girl and they walked away, and I was just standing there, totally dumbfounded for a while, wondering what I did to deserve that."

"Hey, I mean, I would be wondering the same thing. That couldn't have been the best feeling in the world."

"Well that feeling hasn't gone away, honestly," he said. "I still wish people would be a little more grateful sometimes."

Only a few of the stories from our sessions legitimately made me wonder what the hell was wrong with humanity, and this was one them. I could understand some of the reasons why his woman, whomever she was, chose not to express gratitude toward Charles in that moment, but certainly not all of the reasons. It was an example of how strained, to put it mildly, the relationship between African-Americans and the police has become in recent years, and still is to an immense degree. It's clear that relations are getting better as the years progress, but nevertheless, hate and mistrust remain, simultaneously dormant and rampant. It will be the how, where, when, and why of an ending to it all which will be some of the biggest unanswered questions of this American century.

Chapter Seven

"Empathy is key, my friend"

"So, I'll put out a warning for this story beforehand, I know I told you about this one already, so it probably won't be as shocking now, but for people who are reading it for the first time, all I'll say is to be ready for a gruesome event. It might be too demented for most people to comprehend, because even me, being a cop for twenty years, I could barely even comprehend myself what was going on at the scene."

"Noted," I said.

"So, here we go. Dispatch puts out a run for a man barricaded in his apartment, keeping his wife in there, and he's apparently cutting himself with a knife. A pretty dangerous situation, possible domestic violence, probably alcohol or drugs involved, so I'm getting there as fast as I possibly can. A fellow officer had responded with me as well, a younger officer, he was sent to back me up, and we get to the top of the stairs in the apartment building, and we then knock on the door, but in response we could hear him yelling and screaming at us, telling us to go away, and so we tried to kick the door down to start with, but it would not budge, and that was when we realized he was leaning against it."

"Damn, he must have been strong," I commented.

"Well it wasn't necessarily that he was strong, but you'll see why in a minute. So, it took two of us to push the door open just enough for me to get a quarter of my body in, and just the top of my body, my right arm, my head and neck and right shoulder basically. And I look and see him leaning against the door, wearing a pair of shorts and nothing else, and he has cut himself on the arms, his torso, legs, and he's still doing this while I'm trying to talk him down. I'm telling him, you know, 'What are you doing, stop, put the knife down, why are you cutting yourself?' And at this point I could tell he was extremely high, he's so methed out that he's not even acknowledging my presence at that point, other than, when I try to grab his arm he reached up and sliced me on the hand with one of the knives."

"Shit, were you okay?"

"Yeah I was fine, but really that was the least of my worries at that point. I have to figure out what I'm going to do to resolve this, you can't shoot a guy and kill him to keep him from killing himself, right, so your options are really minimal, and talking did not work. So your whole first step of verbal commands, negotiation, talking, it's all out the window, and I can't even get a full body in there to use hands and fists and legs to get to the next step, which is use of force. So, we have to jump straight to the stick."

"The stick?"

"Yep, as officers, some of us will carry a long stick made of cocoaboa wood, it doesn't bend, it doesn't break, it breaks bones. It's used in close quarters situations when a violent suspect needs to be disabled so we can apprehend him. So, my only option really is to try and take out his weapon delivery system, which are his arms, so I grab the stick out of my waistband and hit him in the arm several times, and it breaks his arms in several places. Then, in response to this new development, he switches from his right arm to his left arm, and I couldn't take the chance of hitting him anywhere else, hitting him in the head, hitting him in any red zones that would kill him, so I pause for a second. And after he switches hands, while looking me in the eyes, he literally stopped and looked up at me and looked me in the eye, he began to gut himself like a deer. He went from below the navel, all the way up to his chest bone, his breast bone, and reached in, and started pulling out his intestines. Still looking me in the eye. And I'm hearing this squishing sound while he's pulling his guts out, literally reminds me of field dressing a deer during deer season, same sound, same smell, he's pulling them out, pulls out about seven or eight feet, cuts it off and throws them across the room at his screaming wife. At this point, we had nothing left but to take the hinges out of the door, so I pushed with every ounce of strength I had, my partner put his back against the railing outside the door and pushed with his feet, pushed enough to expose the hinges, pushed hard enough to knock out the pins, and so the door finally gave way and collapsed on top of him. And, he's still got knives with him, but we literally just collapse onto this door on top of him, try to keep him from stabbing himself even more. A third officer is standing in the window of the apartment with a gun, a little bit late, but he saw what happened and was throwing up outside. The guy, he's so methed out that he doesn't know what happening, but finally he stops cutting himself, and me and the younger officer, we get him up off the ground and get him to the squad. And he lived, the guy lived!"

"What the hell, how did he live after all that?" I was incredulous.

"Yeah, cut out his intestines, and lived. Whoever sewed him up did a damn good job. So that was another image I have retained in my brain forever, a guy cutting out his fucking intestines while looking me in the eye. After I broke his arm in two places. It's incredible to think about. Causing that much pain to yourself, nobody can really do that to themselves and live to tell the tale, because they stop when the pain sensors kick in, but this guy was so drugged up, methed out, that his brain just couldn't comprehend what was going on when he was gutting himself."

"That's insane."

"No one in this world should have to go through what I did, to have to see it, write up a report about it, and maintain those images in your brain for the rest of your life. No one, no citizen should have to go through that."

I hit the stop button. It felt like a natural place to end the recording, and it certainly seemed to be time for a smoke break after that ordeal. I stayed inside and went into the kitchen to get us both a glass of water, all the while I continued to process the previous story in my brain, which was manufacturing and transporting images of this man cutting into himself across the stomach in brief flashes throughout my conscious mind. I couldn't quite put an entire scene together, but that would probably come later. It was all a part of my effort to put myself in Charles' place, and to understand how continuous exposure to pain, suffering, and horror can affect an officer.

After he came back inside, we resumed once more, with a couple more stories on the agenda for the day. In case the theme of this session hadn't been clear before, Charles made a point of mentioning it in the beginning of his monologue.

"Another scenario that makes you think to yourself, 'what in the heck is wrong with America, or what is wrong with the world,' because it's not just America where this happens, it happens like this, all over the world. And what I'm talking about are the people and the places where drugs take over and destroy people's lives. Here I responded to what would normally be something like a 'rolling domestic in a car,' but this one was a walking domestic, and this couple, a husband and wife, were walking up the street from a known crack area, where the dealers stand out on the curbs and on stoops of buildings and in alleyways, a place that has almost been abandoned by society in general."

I nodded.

"So, they were coming down the street, someone had called about them yelling and screaming at each other, and I stopped them while they were still arguing with each other, separated them, and talked to them one at a time to try and find out what was going on. You could tell that the man, he was high as a kite, she was kind of, I guess, suffering from not being high as a kite, and she looked a bit disheveled, and I wondered why, stains on the front of her clothes, pants almost falling off her. So, I talked to her first, and from what she was telling me, I figured out that the husband had traded his wife for twenty dollars-worth of crack, and let three dealers have sex with her while he smoked the crack."

"What, seriously?" I was skeptical.

"And she wasn't even mad about that, that actually wasn't the reason they were arguing. She was mad that he hadn't saved her half of the crack for when she got done! And I'm looking at her, just all roughed up and dirty from being I guess on the ground in an alleyway, and she's not even mad about being sold by her husband, she's mad because he didn't share the crack. And it's one of those cases where you just go 'What in the fuck is going on in this world?' Like, have we lost our way? So I talked to him, the husband, and I was like 'This is your wife, man, what are you doing?' And he says 'You don't know man, you don't even have a clue what it's like,' and I mean maybe I didn't, but I do know that I wouldn't trade my wife for a substance. You know?"

"Seems like a basic standard decency between a husband and wife, I would say," I responded.

"You would think!" Charles exclaimed. "Well, it turned out that this guy actually had warrants, so we ended up arresting him for his warrants, and she got sent on her way, going God knows where after that. What was crazy about that whole situation to me was that the wife was willing to go along with it, that's what I couldn't believe. In over twenty years on the force dealing with domestic violence cases and domestic disturbances, I've seen husbands do some terrible, evil things to their wives, but this one had to take the crazy trophy."

"For sure."

"And here's another one will just piss you right off probably, make you think, 'How can it be getting so bad in America that people are living like this,' but it's all true, and it's shameful really given the rich society that we are. So, we're in an area on the west side of the city, a very low-income area, and we're responding, me and another officer, to a call from a house that we've been to a bunch of times, and we know who we're dealing with, pretty much call them by name when we get there. So we knock on the door and we ask the female head of household, by name, what's going on, and she says "Well, the son of a bitch stole my last tv dinner." And it was the only thing they had to eat in the house, for everybody, and in my head I'm like, 'Okay, they called us over that?' But as soon as I had that thought, I also thought, you know, if it is all they had to eat, and they didn't have a whole hell of a lot of money, then you can see why they were arguing over it. And you're trying to come up with a solution that's best for the situation."

"Wait so, who was the one who stole the frozen dinner?" I asked.

"That was the son, he was the tv dinner culprit. He was a teenager, he was a growing boy, so he was probably beside himself starving. The state of the house though was just not an appropriate environment for raising children, there was clutter everywhere, it was a mess everywhere, there's roaches on the wall, and roaches on the furniture, and you're looking around assessing everything, the kitchen is a disaster, dirty dishes and more roaches, but then something even nastier than all of that catches my eye. I kept looking at the play pen that was nearby, and it had puppies inside, dog shit in little piles, and right in one corner of the play pen there was a baby curled up in the corner of it. A baby. An infant. And at this point I don't know whether to feel empathy, or to be pissed off, you know, as a father my brain was just trying to process what I was seeing. But that's not why you're there, you're not there to pass judgement on why their life is the way it is, you're there to answer the call and figure out what's going on and to come up with a solution to their problem."

"Which, when you get right down to it, the problem was that they didn't have enough food," I said.

"Right. I mean the living conditions within the home, the mess and the roaches, it was definitely something I reported later on, and those weren't the worst home conditions I had ever seen, but it was definitely up there. So, as I'm looking over at this play pen and I'm trying to get my partner's attention to that situation, he was saying to me, 'Hey, look at this.' And I look over, and there was literally a dog bed moving across the floor on its own, moving across the living room floor in front of the couch. And even though I knew what the reason behind this trickery was, and I really didn't want to see it, I went over and flipped the bed over with my stick, and about a hundred cockroaches took off in every direction, and they had literally been carrying the bed across the floor as they were moving. So I'm seeing human feces, dog feces, the family arguing over that little bit of food, a dog bed moving on its own from bug infestations, children in deplorable conditions, and you know, is arresting either one of the parents at that point going make a difference?"

"Arresting them for child endangerment? Probably not."

Charles nodded.

"It really wouldn't have helped the whole situation if I had done that. I mean, you have to report them through the appropriate channels, get an investigation started, and go from there, but taking the mom away right then would have made things go from bad to worse. And the meanwhile, what do you do? So, I go over to the mom and pull her aside, and I took twenty dollars out of my pocket, and I said look, go buy some food. And then tried to reinforce with the son, which we did and she did, that the food was for everyone, and it can't be just ate up in one sitting, because you know, they're trying to get through to their next monthly check, and that resolved it for the day, but I mean, we went back later. And that's the problem, you know, once you show that empathy and you reach into your own pocket, then eventually they come to expect that. And we get a call for some other reason the next week, can't even remember what the purpose of the visit had been, but in reality, the only purpose was to get us to come and give them money again. And you know, I'm not made of money, cops don't make a lot of money at all, it's more of a heart thing than a money thing, but you can't help them every time. You try and help out as much as you can, though, you don't want anybody going hungry or cold, but there did end up being an investigation, and the house ended up being condemned, and they had to make them move out to a different place, to a cleaner and more well-maintained apartment with the children, one where the landlords would not let the place get to the state that their previous home had been in, or they had let it become. So that was a lot healthier for the children, and I was glad to see it, and I hate to think that I had them displaced but really there was just no way those kids were going to have a chance if they had stayed in the other place. The house was torn down eventually, and we responded to their next problems at a different location, and it continued on."

I heaved a sigh.

"Well, good on you for helping them out a little. It's sad that it created a kind of dependence on their part, but I mean, what are you going to do, let them starve?"

"Exactly, you have to have some empathy in those situations. But sometimes there's not much you can do to change these people's lives so that they don't have to be dependent, whether it's through lack of will, or just being stuck in a rut and not knowing how to get out of it, you'll have people who are always going to be in the dregs of society. People just can't seem to break out of these terrible conditions. We're going from dealing with entire families over the course of just a couple decades, and I've seen it. One day we're dealing with grandpa and his problems, and then we have to arrest the son, and then his son, down to the great grand-children, same family committing the same crimes in the same cycle over and over."

That notion really floored me, I have to admit.

"But how do you solve that?" I asked, with a sense of exasperation. "I mean, I think that in America we talk about generational poverty all the time, but it doesn't seem like a lot of headway has been made, at least in my lifetime. Was this situation in particular solely a parenting issue in your mind, like was the mother just someone who really shouldn't have had kids?" I probed.

Charles took a deep breath, and paused to think.

"Well, I mean, you can say that, but at the end of the day, ultimately, I think the old saying that it takes a village to raise a child, I think that fits that situation well. Of course, the foundations start in the home, and at school, but the sad thing is that a lot of the people we were dealing with don't know how to be parents, because their parents didn't know how to be parents, or they were young when they got pregnant and didn't have a lot of support, or they were on drugs, so it is a cycle and it is incredibly difficult to stop. So part of it is certainly generational, you're right. You continue to respond to the same problem with different people, or the same people with different problems, and they can't help it because that was how they were raised and that was how they raised their kids and nobody ever told them any different. Really, it's only half their fault, the other half of the blame is society and our communities, we've failed these people on a societal level in certain respects."

That gave me a lot to think about.

"I think you're exactly right. I mean, I study public policy and government in school, and the problem is that it takes a huge amount of political will to spend money on programs that will help people like that family. People think they don't deserve it because they say they're lazy and will always be dependent and will have no incentive to make positive changes in their lives. And that may be true in certain circumstances, but my take is, Charles, that if you don't actually give people the chance to change in the first place, or facilitate the conditions for change, then you're really just giving them nowhere else to turn. You're giving them no choice but to be dependent and have to live in terrible conditions and live off the government, and commit crimes. But we can't help them unless we help them. And I like that village metaphor. I think we as villagers need to step up and be more empathic and supporters of our fellow citizens."

Charles nodded.

"I agree. Empathy is the key, my friend, you can't have hate in your heart, you can't have contempt. Especially as a cop, you're a public servant, and that means protecting and serving everyone," he said.

"Well, if you don't mind me asking, what other types of situations did you encounter on the job where you just shook your head and said, you know, 'I can't believe people are living like this' or where you just wanted to scream at people and knock some sense into them, but you couldn't?"

"Oh, plenty," Charles responded. "Like I said, I'd seen worse conditions than that house before, there were hoarders who hadn't put their trash out to the curb in years, and there would be literally no place to even move around inside the house except for like, a path to the bedroom and the refrigerator, and the smell was just awful, so we would have to get the health department involved and sometimes get the person evaluated. But as far as other living situations, the mom in that house didn't work, no one worked, they depended on government checks to survive. Other times, you've got a single mom, doesn't know who the father of her baby is, so she's working and doing what she can to raise the child, bringing home dudes just to help out and pay some of the bills. It's a repeated story, over and over again."

"You know, you would hope that we could solve problems like those through everybody's combined efforts, the friends, neighbors, the police, the government. It does truly take a village. It seems like there are a lot of resources and institutions that are ready to help. The state, non-profits, the Church."

Charles interjected.

"Well you want to say the Church, but unfortunately I don't think I can say church."

"Not anymore?" I asked.

"No, people are losing faith, they're losing their humanity, their slaves to their phones, you know, as we sit here both with our phones right next to us. The church, whatever denomination you are, is usually a force for good in the community, but it is a shell of its former self in my opinion. People just aren't empathetic anymore, it goes back to empathy again and again. No one has the heart, no one prays anymore, no one looks at a stranger and sees a potential friend, they just automatically see an enemy. No one looks at the downtrodden and thinks about what they can do to help, they just ignore them."

"It's sad. We're all guilty of it."

"All of us. No one is without blame for these problems."

"But how do you fix it?"

"I don't know brother, I truly don't know." He pointed to me. "That's up to your generation, that's up to you guys."

I laughed a little bit in response.

"Yeah, we're working on it. I think the situation gets better as the years go on, but the challenges change as well, the challenges seem to morph and evolve even as society makes headway on some of these poverty issues. There's always going to be a new and different problems to face," I propounded.

"I agree," Charles said.

Chapter Eight

"From a law enforcement perspective"

"You know, can I tell you something?"

We were about to settle in for another session, same time as always and same place. I had called to order a barbeque chicken pizza a few minutes before he walked in the door, so we would have some delicious lunch to enjoy in short order. By this point in my journey as Charles' biographer, our interviews were becoming a routine, but there was no less of an enthusiasm from either of us for the task at hand. I like to think that we had grown as individuals as compared to when we first began. At least, I know I had. Charles and I had become good friends, and he even took to calling me 'partner' all the time, like he would one of his fellow officers. And I could see why, given the nature of our undertaking. He was entrusting me with the details of his life story, putting his faith and trust in me as a writer to translate the lessons he had learned as a police officer to the general public. That was what our project was supposed to be about. Letting people know that cops aren't so different from you and me, from a regular citizen. In fact, they're not different at all. They are ordinary people who are tasked with confronting the oftentimes terrible realities of everyday life in our society.

"Yeah sure, what's up?"

"I just want to say thank you for everything you're doing, helping me put this book together, and also that I really hope we can change some minds when people read it. Some people's minds aren't going to change, but I hope that some will. You'll never know how much I appreciate all the work you're putting into this."

I nodded in acknowledgement.

"Well, I'm learning a lot myself through this process, it's opening my eyes to things that I would not have been aware of if I hadn't met you. So yeah, hey, it's no problem at all. It's been a great ride so far."

"It has."

"I know some of it has been difficult for you, recounting some of these memories that are painful, but I think people just need to understand the reality out there."

"Exactly."

For that day's interview, we had decided to focus on 'the issues,' and by that, I mean the polarizing social and political concerns which everyone has the right to have an opinion about, but no one can claim to have all the answers to the questions which they elicit. I thought it would be valuable to add a law enforcement perspective to a certain few of these debates, and Charles agreed.

"So, what do we have on the list as far as the issues?" he asked.

I looked down at my journal.

"We've got a lot to cover, that's for sure. I vote we start with drugs, might as well take a look at that seeing as heroin is out of control right now and there doesn't seem to be anything we can do about it."

Charles launched right into a speech, catching me off guard, but I had enough time to start the recording before I missed anything important.

"Right. So, let's talk about heroin, the epidemic of heroin. It's not just local, it's not just cities, its everywhere, and during the later stages of my career, we were coming to a point where NARCAN was the answer to the problem, and they were wanting to put it in police officer's hands, so that as we responded to emergencies we could administer the NARCAN, and assume that people are having a heroin overdose if they show certain symptoms. I mean let's be honest, we're not medical professionals, we have CPR training and I had combat medic training, but when it comes to differentiating between different types of medical emergencies, you know, that's a lot of knowledge and responsibility to put on a cop."

"Definitely."

"So, I've got a good one for you, and hopefully this might help people understand what we dealt with as cops when it comes to all of these overdoses. It was a normal morning in the city, the day had been pretty quiet up to that point, and as I pull on to one of our main thoroughfares, there's a box truck in front of me which suddenly sideswipes a telephone pole and then takes off through the red light at the intersection he was about to come up on. So I lit him up, closed in on him, but he wasn't going very fast though, he was driving kind of erratic and all over the road. After about eight or so blocks, going about ten miles per hour, all of the sudden he pulls over and stops. So I'm going up cautiously, don't know quite what the situation is at this point, is he really high on something, is he really drunk, is there a medical emergency, I couldn't really tell exactly what was going on by the way he was driving. I've got my hand on my gun just in case, and I approach the car to try and see what's going on with this guy. Then as I conduct the stop, this guy is combative verbally, and he opens his car door and tries to have a go at us."

"There was another cop with you?" I asked.

"Yeah, I had radioed for backup when he swiped the telephone pole, just thought it might be a potentially dangerous stop. So, me and my fellow officer are about to put him on the ground and restrain him, but then we notice as we're kind of tangling with him that he's not quite right. He's sweating profusely, he's confused, just out of his mind confused, talking nonsense, and something just clicked in my brain at that moment. Our first reaction was that he was overdosing, and the outward symptoms pointed in that direction somewhat. But as we were trying to check him out and stabilize him, for some reason I thought, 'This doesn't seem like heroin.' He's delirious, talking gibberish, and there would have been slightly different symptoms if he had been overdosing."

"Like what?" I asked.

"Things like weak breathing, losing consciousness in and out, sometimes their lips will be blue from oxygen loss, and the pupils will be extremely small, that's another sign of an overdose. But this guy, it just looked different, if it had been a heroin overdose, he probably wouldn't have been able to drive as well as he did, you know, stop his car, and even stand upright, it would have been very obvious that he was close to death's door if it had been heroin. So, instead of getting more physical with him, you know instead of throwing him on the ground and restraining him, we led him around to the curb and sat him next to a pole, and I started to try to get him to come around and focus on me and what I was saying. And after about a thousand times of asking, "Are you a diabetic? Are you a diabetic?" he finally answers yes, and so, one of the other officers was looking through the cabin of his truck, and I asked him if there was insulin in the car, and he said yes. So, we got in the car and looked and his lunchbox was in there, and inside was a needle, and then when we see that, we're going 'Oh shit, maybe we're wrong,' but underneath the needle, thank God, was a bottle of insulin. So when the squad got there, they administered the insulin to him and basically saved his life. So there, we had an insulin dependent diabetic having an emergency, which could very easily be confused for a heroin overdose."

"Obviously then, giving him NARCAN wouldn't have really done anything, right?" I asked.

"Exactly, he might have died right there if we hadn't recognized that he was having a diabetic emergency. An officer who doesn't maybe have as much medical training as I do might not be aware of what to do in that kind of situation, and you know, might end up having the death of someone who really needed insulin on their hands. At the time, there were a lot of officers out there, myself included, I won't lie, who thought that having the NARCAN in our cars would become a liability. Because you can get sued by the family of someone if you make an on the spot diagnosis of an emergency like that and you end up being wrong. But we ended up getting it put in there, so now every cop has a supply of NARCAN with them in case of overdoses, which, as we all know, are very frequent nowadays."

Charles paused as if he had run out of things to say, and so I consulted my list of questions I had prepared for this session to see what other direction we could take the conversation.

"And well, something I think we can add to this story is your opinion on illegal drugs. I think we can all agree that heroin should not be legal, it's clearly a menace to society, but what about everything else, running up the ladder from marijuana to cocaine to pills, other types of recreational drugs?"

"Okay, yeah we can talk about that. So let's look at crack cocaine, since we already looked at opiates. It started back in the 1990's, when doctors were giving out pain medication for pretty much anything, and then they would just take people off it if they showed signs of dependency. And the pills on the street were ungodly expensive, like forty to fifty dollars each, and so the cheapest, next best opiate was to go to heroin. Some people would go to crack, because you know that's the cheapest way to get that high using cocaine. So those drugs, you know, this was a created problem, this was somebody seizing the opportunity to satisfy people's needs for opiates, they saw that this was going to be a big sale. But now there's a whole new deal, it's gotten so rampant and widespread that it's become a part of the fabric of our nation unfortunately. People are trying to combat the problem, but it's just grown absolutely out of control. You've got people going to the hospital to get methadone, and two floors up there is someone in chronic pain with a chronic disease or disability who can't get it as often as they need it. And a lot of the guys who are getting methadone, well some of the guys, not all of them, will sell the methadone that they get and then use that money to buy heroin. And then they'll overdose."

"Wow. That's healthy," I commented. "And then you add fentanyl in the mix too."

"Yeah, it's bad. We had heroin come in one week that was cut with rat poison, and when we discovered this, we really didn't have a choice, we had to go out and warn the people who we knew were addicts to not to buy this stuff, because we knew it was going to get them killed. But, so, in answer to your question, I don't think any opiates or cocaine should be legalized recreationally. Marijuana is obviously a different story. Every domestic violence call I ever went to, and I've been to a lot, most domestic incidents are caused by either mental illness, mental issues like anger problems, and being empowered by alcohol. Alcohol is always recurring theme in domestic violence calls. Marijuana smokers, they might be pissed that the pizza man is late, but they're not beating on each other, they're not going crazy as a result of using the drug. If they smoke in their house, everything's fine, just don't smoke out on the streets in front of the cops because then they will do something, but it's just a citation. Until it gets legalized of course, which I think it inevitable really, but I guess that's an issue that's out of my hands."

"Sounds good to me," I said, satisfied with his answers. It was exactly what I had expected him to say.

"I think that's a position on marijuana that a lot of people probably share," I offered. "I mean, it's a plant, right? And as long as it's regulated and taxed properly, I don't know if I see too much of a downside. And the medicinal benefits can't be ignored."

"Exactly," Charles responded. "I really wish Ohio would get around to legalizing it soon. You know about the pain I struggle with from my surgeries, I would love to try it out, see how it could help me. It's an everyday thing for me, and the bottle I get prescribed only has so many pills in it. I'm going through the exact same thing that a lot of the addicts out there are going through, and it sucks, man. And a lot of the homeless vets who are addicted to drugs or drink too much, a lot of that is because they probably had some terrible injury while serving, and, whether they didn't get it treated properly or whatever the case might be, they have to medicate somehow, and it ends up destroying them. I can't tell you enough how much it affects you when you have chronic pain. You want to get rid of it at all costs, and some people turn to the harder drugs, because it helps. I hope you don't ever have to deal with what I'm dealing with in your life."

"I hope so too, man, I feel for you."

We adjourned quickly for a break, as Charles headed outside to smoke and I stayed in, busying myself around the apartment, but not really accomplishing much of anything. When he came back inside, I somewhat callously reminded him that the cigarettes were going to kill him eventually. But he didn't seem to mind the admonishment.

"I know they are. I'm going to die anyway, right? Might as well be sooner rather than later," he told me.

Well, that was a depressing statement.

"I guess it might not do a lot of good at this point," I said.

"No, not at all," he responded.

After that exchange, we settled back down at the kitchen table and started up on the recordings again.

"So next, how about gun control?" I asked. "Definitely an issue where I think a cop would have something valuable to add to the debate."

"Sure, let's do gun control. What do we want to say about it?"

"Well I guess just tell me your opinion on it from a law enforcement perspective, and then follow up with what you personally think about the second amendment, and then maybe from a legal standpoint, we can discuss some common-sense laws that should be passed to try and prevent, or well, at least lower the chances of more of these mass shootings happening in America."

"Okay, sounds good." Charles paused for a moment, gathering his thoughts. "I've actually got a good story that relates to gun control if you want to hear it, just about some people we had to deal with who were trying to use the second amendment as an excuse to carry around huge guns and would try to sue people who harassed them."

I raised my eyebrows.

"Yeah go ahead with it, whatever experiences you had will be valuable for people to read about," I said.

Charles cleared his throat.

"So, gun control, from the point of view of a police officer. In the state of Ohio where we live, it's an open carry state, and there are a lot of guys out there who are trying to get their point across, you know, they're the crazy second amendment pushing people, which, you know, I believe in the second amendment and I own guns, but I am aware of how to use them responsibly, but there are some people in this world who can't, for whatever reason. And some people, there are other people, who are just trying to make a big show, and are just trying to get attention, and for police officers in particular, they're trying to get us to react and do something wrong, so they can sue you and sue the city you work for."

"That's kind of, uh, not nice," I responded.

"Well, these weren't people with the highest of moral character, if you know what I mean. So, we would get an abundance of these calls, more than you would probably think. One guy we had a run in with, this was someone who apparently had been doing this very frequently, and in other areas, just not in our jurisdiction until then, and he was walking down the street with a rifle slung over his shoulder, and it was like an M1 Garand or something, just a very dangerous looking gun, strapped over his shoulder, walking down the street in broad daylight. So obviously we get about a thousand calls, 'man with a big gun walking down the street,' 'man with a rifle,' and that's what he's looking for, right? He's looking for you to point your gun at him, to scream and yell at him, to put him on the ground, you know, and he's hoping that he's going get arrested, but of course, it's not against the law, it's an open carry state, and if you have an open carry permit, that's what your allowed to do."

I was taken aback by the scenario he was describing, and just the gall of these people to take advantage of other people's sense of security so selfishly.

"So, they make sure that they have it strapped over their shoulder, it's not pointed at anybody, it's not threatening anybody, it's just there in plain view for everyone in the community to see. And you have to approach these people with caution, you can't just go gung-ho at them, you have to very cautiously start to approach them, and be ready for whatever might happen. How we would do it, we would just approach them by striking up a conversation. For example, 'Hey, that's a great looking rifle, I've got one just like it' or something like that. Usually they will ignore these attempts at conversation, and then after a few tries at getting them into a dialogue, they'll say something like 'You're harassing me,' and we'll say, 'No we're not.' Or they'll say, 'Well I'm not doing anything wrong,' and we'll say back, 'Well, you might be or you might not be, we need to see your open carry permit to make sure.' So you just had to walk on eggshells with these guys, their goal was to get you to say something, a lot of times they have like a voice-activated recorder in their pocket, or they got their buddy recording it from the other side of the street with a cell phone."

I had only ever heard of this kind of behavior once or twice on the news, so I was kind of surprised at how much he said it had happened, in just one city no less. I decided to ask him about the frequency of those kinds of encounters.

"So did this happen a lot during your career?"
Charles nodded.

"These guys were in abundance, once it started getting warm out every year we'd start getting the calls. Towards the end of my career in 2016 it slowed down a little bit, but you still see them around every so often, people with holsters with desert eagles in them, just big crazy guns and people trying to be cowboys, walking down the street with a .45 long rifle, and you know, they have to understand that there's limits."

"There's freedom, but all freedom has its limits."

"It has its limits, it has its boundaries, and these were the people who pushed the boundaries. They can carry their gun in public, but they can also be seen as a menace to society and be seen as disturbing the peace. And businesses are allowed to make their own rules about firearms on their premises, so they can't be on the premises of a business which doesn't allow open carry. It becomes a matter of respect then too, respect for your fellow man, not inducing panic, not trespassing. So basically, they targeted the main streets then, they target the most public places possible, just to try and get a rise out of the public, and a rise out of us. The issue became separating politics from danger."

"I can see that, yeah."

The conversation came to a natural end, but I was still upset, at least in my own head, about the people who were on the streets doing this. They gave legitimately responsible gun owners a bad name. I own guns because I enjoy shooting them, and our family keeps several in our home for the sake of personal protection and self-defense, in deference to the remotest possibility for any kind of situation or event which might cause the need for it. That was it. I was sure that Charles felt the same way, but it still frustrated me that people were out there doing that, using their guns in such a socially irresponsible and also morally reprehensible manner.

We got up to refill our waters in the kitchen, and we just talked for a couple minutes about our guns, making tentative plans to go shooting together at some point in the near future, maybe when all of this was said and done. Our lunch had finally arrived as well, and so I got us out some plates and napkins and we started eating. Sitting back down, I knew we had a lot more to talk about on this subject, and while we were eating, I thought about further directions I could steer our gun control conversation.

After about fifteen minutes or so, I started up another dialogue for us.

"So, people are allowed to carry their guns in public in Ohio, but there are certain places where you can't have guns, certain common sense places, but in the case of all these school shootings, to use a very important example, some of these are cases where the shooters got the guns they used from their parents, took them, and decided to bring them to school one day. I mean, there's no way to stop that, and have the second amendment at the same time."

"We have to have the second amendment, I wholeheartedly believe in our rights as Americans to own and use firearms," Charles said. "It's what makes us a really hard country to invade in the case of a land war."

For some reason I burst out laughing when he said that, mostly because it was a true statement.

Charles was bemused at my response.

"Well it's the truth. You hope that we don't have another world war in the future, but in case the conflict ever hits our shores, you know, try invading and taking over West Virginia. That would be worse than the Russian winter."

That made me laugh even harder.

"I guess, man."

"Back to the second amendment, though," Charles said.

"Yeah, back to the second amendment."

"So, with the second amendment, the question is, how do you protect our rights and try and stop some of these school shootings and mass shootings from happening in the future."

"Without outright banning guns."

"Right. Well, the easy answer is that there's no easy answer. From a law enforcement perspective, the less guns out on the street, the easier our job is, and so we're trying to get guns out of the hands of people who are going to be using them to commit crimes or murder or what have you. But that still doesn't solve the school shooting problem, I think the school shooting problem is only going to be solved with time, with parents being more responsible with their firearms, and with an increased emphasis on identifying persons who are at risk of perpetrating that kind of horrific crime."

I nodded my head. "I do agree with the need for a greater emphasis on mental health in our society, but again, it's still difficult to gauge someone's mental health during a background check. It's a difficult balance, to protect individual rights, and to protect the public at the same time."

"It is," said Charles, "that's a tough question."

I continued.

"And all those cases where the shooter took the guns from their parents' gun safe because they told their kids the passcode, that probably would have made it harder for those people to commit those crimes if they hadn't had easy access to the rifles and ammo their parents owned. And that's not even to mention the cases where the guns were just out in the open and the parents didn't have them locked up."

"Yes, the irresponsible parents in those cases, not good at all," Charles responded. "For us as police officers, we do what we can, we take illegal guns off the street, but the legal guns, that's a different question. I don't know what the answer to that question is…"

He was silent for a few moments, and I couldn't think of anything to say either.

"The school shootings themselves, though, if and when they do happen, we can prepare for those, prepare for what we would do if we find ourselves as a responding officer in that kind of terrible situation," he elaborated.

"Oh, so did you guys have drills for school shootings that you practiced?" I asked.

"Of course, we would have active shooter drills all the time, and training for those types of events, and some of them we did do on the premises of the local schools to imitate if it happened in real life. And let me tell you, they were intense, man."

"I'm sure."

"We had a drill modeled after the Columbine shooting that we did every couple years, with a hypothetical scene at a high school, where you're responding to reports of gunshots at the school, someone is heavily armed and shooting kids, shooting teachers. And in this scenario, you are either the school resource officer or a police officer who is at the school that day, or an officer who is in the vicinity, and you are the first to respond. We all have keycards to get into all the schools, so if you are there or nearby, you aren't waiting for backup, you have to go. Lives are at stake."

"Definitely. Can you tell me about the drill?" I prompted.

"Sure thing. So, as you enter the building you hear shots being fired, you don't know where they're coming from, but you know they're close. You hear people screaming, and so your weapon is drawn and you're moving tactically down the hallways towards the sounds. At this point, you're already ramped up, your anxiety is through the roof, brain and body are stressed, and all of the sudden, a kid runs out in front of you. You got a half a second to decide, is that a shooter or is that a kid just running away? You ascertain the situation, see that it's just a kid who's scared out of his mind or scared out of her mind, so you tell them to find a hiding place or find the nearest exit, and then you move on, go, go, go. The shooting continues. You come around the corner, and you see the shooter. At that moment, you have all the burdens in your mind coming to a head. You see that he's a threat, but then you're thinking who is this kid? Whose kid is he, why is he doing this, and you know that you can't value his life over the ones he's killing, and so you have to stop him, you have to engage him, and that's all there is to it. You potentially have to kill a kid, who might be the same age as one of my own kids, which just makes the training even more real."

"Yeah, I never thought about that."

"You will when you have kids of your own. So then, you engage with the shooter, he's in the middle of shooting a bunch of people, you get a shot off, and the shooter goes down. You've neutralized one threat. But then as you approach the kid you've just shot, you continue to hear screams and more gunshots, so you have to assume there is a second shooter. The problem is, you can't just leave that kid you just shot, you don't know if he's mortally wounded, if he's going to get back up and start shooting people again, but you don't have time to stop and cuff him, it's just you at that point, so what do you do? The decision is right in front of you, but it not something that anybody should have to be put in the position to do. You can't bring yourself to put another round in the kid you just shot to make sure he stays down and doesn't kill more people, so you kick his primary weapon away and hope he doesn't have more on his person, and you advance down the hall towards the sounds of the second shooter. You engage with the second shooter in the same manner, you hopefully have the time to cuff and secure the second shooter, and then you can go back and secure the first kid."

"Wow. That's a lot of terrible decisions to make in a situation like that," I reacted.

"For sure, it is," he responded. "We always have to prepare for the worst, and that includes the training to know what to do in those types of situations."

"And you know, at the risk of stating the obvious, it just highlights how difficult the job of a police officer can be, for not a great deal of compensation. Seems like the general public might be a little more sympathetic if they understood the truly wide range of responsibilities that cops have in our society," I offered.

"I would definitely hope so," Charles responded.

"So, I mean, that's a good transition into what I wanted our next topic to be, which is exactly what I was just saying about public perception," I said. "I guess I just want to get some unfiltered opinion from you about that. Like, what are the things that you most want the public to know about the police? The job that cops do, and what really goes on behind the scenes and behind the media portrayals."

I paused quickly, to develop the question a bit further before he could answer.

"And also, what do you want to say in response to some of the negative impressions that people may have about who you are and what it is you do for a living?"

I will admit that this conversation was, to a greater degree, more choregraphed than all our previous interviews, at least on my end. Especially for this chapter, I wanted to structure the dialogue so I could uncover *exactly* what he thought about the general public's perception of him, and of the police in general. Not that he had ever been indirect before, or camouflaged his true beliefs, but I knew that asking the right questions would enable me to better understand his thoughts on these issues.

"Well," Charles began, "if there's one big thing I want people to understand, it's that, in this world of media sensationalism, the media in general has... Now, they're not entirely at fault for it, but they have their share of the responsibility, for segregating our communities, for portraying the police as antagonists within their communities, for overwhelmingly covering the stories that make us look bad and not the ones that show that we're just human. And just generally for making our job more difficult in terms of community relations. The desire of the media to put out the most shocking and terrible stories that have to do with the police, to focus on the negatives, oftentimes without even having all the facts right, does not help us in doing our job."

"So a lot of it is the media for you, news and television?" I asked.

"Like I said, not all of it, but they certainly don't help. And yes I know, it has to do with profits, with getting more people to watch or to click on a story or whatever, but at the end of the day, let me tell you, I think it does way more harm than good."

I nodded.

"So, just playing devil's advocate here, but someone, in response to that, might say that media exposure to the bad behavior of police officers serves the purpose of holding them accountable for their actions, sort of like a public shaming which discourages other officers from repeating the same bad behaviors. What would you say to that?" I queried.

"Well I would agree with that, but only to a certain extent. We need to weed out the bad cops, the ones who are doing the job for the wrong reasons, the ones who are racist or who are just going out there waiting to pound somebody's head in, but also, here's the thing, if you're constantly putting out negative stories about cops, and you make us feel like we're the bad guys, it will eventually have that effect on us, where we actually do go around thinking we're the bad guys, thinking it's a war zone when in reality we have to be community servants, not soldiers. It does something to you psychologically, to be hated by someone, for some guys they might embrace the role of the villain, but we can't have that. Society would fall apart if every cop thought of their communities as a war zone, as an 'us versus them' mentality. That's not good."

"No, it's not."

"So I just want people to know that we aren't the enemy. I'm not doing this job to judge people, to put people down, there's only one who can judge us for our actions, and He is the creator of this Earth, and He is not me. If I haven't walked a mile in your shoes, I can't understand the reason for your actions, I don't know why people do what they do. I refused to pass judgement on the people I dealt with as an officer, because I didn't know what they were dealing with in life. As cops and as citizens we don't take the time to understand the reasons behind people's actions. If they're in the middle of financial hardships, in the middle of a divorce, they've been diagnosed with cancer, they're losing their kids. Yeah maybe this guy is pissed off and he's drunk, and by God he probably should be, you know?"

I laughed at that one.

"Sometimes, you just have to show a little empathy for your neighbor," I said.

Charles nodded.

"As citizens of American society, it's really our duty to show kindness. And let's not forget that the cops are just citizens too, we understand that life is tough. But if you think about us as the enemy, and make us into the enemy, it's going to make us less and less likely to empathize with you. I don't go around wanting to make arrests, wanting to get into fights or risk getting shot. It would be great if everybody in society just got along with each other, but you know, that's the job, that's the real deal. The real deal is you're dealing with disgusting places, bugs, diseases, people who just don't give a fuck about themselves or anybody else, and your brain is infiltrated and convoluted with evil shit that you can't get rid of, and despite everything, you still show up. Even when it got announced that we weren't getting paid for the next month, and that did happen, the city had some budgetary issues for couple years. We still showed up and did the job."

"Of course you did," I said. He hadn't told me about that particular time in his career, but I wasn't surprised about the fact that he still showed up and did the job.

"And on the other side, a note to the cops, guys, we have to live by the laws we enforce. You are not better than anyone else, you are a citizen just like the people in your community, so you cannot be a hypocrite and arrest somebody for a DWI and then go out to a bar after work and drive yourself home and now you're throwing up in the middle of the road. Despite the difficulties of the job, this is what we signed up for, we signed up to be held to higher standard, you are supposed to be a pillar of the community, a bedrock of the community, what holds everybody together. When you're off-duty, every one of your actions is seen by the community. So, we need to get our heads out of our asses, live life on the straight and narrow, right on the blue line, don't fall off it, and do what we're supposed to do as servants to the community."

"That's a good message." I made a couple notes in my journal to myself, about the possibility of elaborating on that message to his fellow officers.

"So then," I continued, "let's talk about the people who are doing the job for the wrong reasons. You know, on the one hand, talking to you has made me think about how all of our public servants deserve to get paid more than they do, for doing the jobs that they do, whether it's teachers, firefighters, the police, they do more work to keep the fabric of our society stitched tightly together than anybody else. But you know, especially with the police, there are always going to be people who join the force without thinking about their true responsibility of being a community servant, a public servant. So, what do you have to say about that? How can we ensure that the people we entrust to be officers of the law are doing it for the right reasons?"

Charles was deep in thought for a few moments.

"So, here's the thing. There are a couple of types of people who become police officers. There are the people who have wanted to be cops since childhood, and some of those people are the perfect candidates, but some are not. Others just want the authority, they want the power, and they join up so they can make the arrests and get the glory. They're so many variables to consider, you have to have the right mentality, you have to be patient, be empathetic, and I think we just have to get better at vetting officers, before they get out onto the street and do more harm than good for their community."

"Well, how do you do that?" I asked.

"There are a couple ways. Now, I was a field training officer, I didn't actually interview anyone for a job, but I was there in the beginning of a lot of young cops' careers, and so to a certain extent, I was able to tell who was going to be a 'good' cop and who was going to be a 'bad' cop, if you want to put it that way. But as an interviewer, you have to ask those important, tough questions, asking the applicants why they want to become a police officer, but also be able to see through the bullshit at the same time. The standards should be very high. You're trusted with a gun, with the ability to make life or death decisions, and only the right kind of people can be trusted to carry out such an important function in the community, to protect and to serve."

"It makes you think about politicians too, right? They should be held to equally high standards, and it begs the question of how we can vet them more than we already do," I expressed.

"That's right, who's going to vet them, the voters have to vet them, but voters can only do so much. A lot of times we get suckered into sensationalism, into a herd mentality, it's us versus them, Republicans versus Democrats, cops versus citizens, whatever it is. Now, we can use our rational thinking abilities as human beings to resist being herded in one direction or another, but I don't have much hope that we can do that anymore. That's what separates us from the animals, we can use our superior brains instead of relying on instinct, but it doesn't look like we're that far removed from our ancestors in a lot of cases."

"You might be right about that. And I think the interesting thing is too, is that the police are on the front lines facing down the people who have to resort to their more animalistic urges, because many people who commit you know, felonies or violent crimes, they're in survival situations, they don't have a choice, they're just doing what they think they need to do to survive."

"That's right, cops are always there for the situations where people are at their lowest, for when they're suffering and they need a way out. It's a wonder why nobody likes us, you know? We always used to say that we only ever deal with good people when we're dealing with victims."

"That's kind of sad to think about," I said.

"It is sad. And our interactions with them were usually very short, because we just had to get enough information to file the report."

We shared silence for about thirty seconds or so as we kept on eating our lunch. I decided to ask him the biggest question that had been on my mind through this entire discussion, one that certainly had, and has, no easy answer.

"So, is there a way to fix all of this, to build a bridge between civilians and the police that will actually, you know, stay up for a while, that will stand the test of time?"

He answered immediately, which surprised me somewhat.

"There are some solutions," Charles began. "Like for example, I think citizens on patrol is good. But we don't have enough of them, that's one problem, and the other problem is that the ages are generally a different generation than the people out there committing crimes unfortunately, usually the people who sign up to be community police officers are older, right, and so we do need younger people to step up into those roles and say, 'hey, we want our communities to be better, so we're going to be examples for others and keep the peace.' But not a lot of young people are willing to do that, or maybe, young people don't even know that that's a volunteer program that they can join."

"I could see that as a breakthrough solution if it is implemented on wide scale," I responded. "It seems like there would have to be a lot of planning and regulations and laws that would have to be passed to make it happen, but I don't see why we can't at least try."

"The problem is that it would be very complicated to put that in every community, and the other problem is that it's even harder to vet the people who sign up to be community volunteer police officers than it is to vet the ones who get paid. The big example that comes to mind is the unfortunate situation that happened down in Florida."

I paused for a second, until I realized what he was talking about.

"Ah, Trayvon."

"Trayvon Martin, yep. And so in light of that terrible tragedy and others like it, if we don't have changes made to the ways even our community policing programs are run, then we could have more incidents like that happen, and that goes back to vetting. Back to square one."

I shook my head, perplexed. But I did have another thought I wanted to run by him.

"Well, here was my other idea, though. As I was thinking a little bit about this before you got here today, of how we could solve this kind of problem where we have to vet people more thoroughly for the job of being a police officer, I also thought about having some kind of degree-granting program for police officers. Paid for by the government, so not only could we have more rigorous training and official standards for potential police officers, but also, people in poor communities who might not have the economic means to go to college could make a career out of criminal justice, and then go back and serve in their own communities if possible. Something like a two-year degree in criminal justice or whatever the name would be, and you take two years to learn how to be a police officer, the right way. You study, you train, you study and train, you take tests, you go out on runs even before you actually go out into the world, you learn how to handle firearms properly, learn the responsibility of having a service weapon, you learn how to respect people. And I think the people who would be joining the police for the wrong reasons would get filtered out by that kind of two-year, rigorous program? Any thoughts on that idea?"

"Yeah, I love it, man. I could definitely see that happening."

We took a break before the final recording we had planned for that session. Charles went out to smoke, and I decided to go out with him this time and indulge in some nicotine myself. He would always tell me, reflecting his characteristic fatalist attitude, that he had no desire to quit smoking, since he felt he might soon die anyway someday soon, from any of the host of ailments he was suffering from in the present or might suffer from in the future. It was his way of coping. He had to laugh about his mortality, otherwise he would probably have to cry about it. There wasn't really much I could do about that myself, other than to laugh and smoke along with him.

"So, you said you wanted to talk about religion also, about your faith, and how your career has been sort of a challenge to your faith and your belief in God. Can you explain all of that for me, what you've had to deal with in terms of your faith during your career?"

"Sure thing. I've been a religious man my entire life, I go to Church every Sunday, and I say that proudly. I'm not perfect by any means, I have my own laundry list of flaws and faults, but I try to make up for it by being kind to my fellow human beings in this crazy thing we call life. But being a police officer has challenged my faith in certain respects, I'll admit it. You've got the family and home situations where people are just totally destitute, can't take care of themselves, can't take care of their children, and it seems like society has forgotten them, and you have to ask, who's fault is that? It's everyone's fault, you can only blame individuals for their own problems up to a point, there are some situations where the blame has to be distributed. So, you wonder, not only where the rest of the community plays a part in taking care of those people and helping them to rise above their circumstances and have a better life, but also where God is in those situations, where prayer plays a role, where the Church might be able to help. It seems like everybody who goes to church now just goes through the motions, and we don't help each other out, and I wonder where the blame lays for that failure in our society. And furthermore, you see all of the senseless death in your career as a cop, the death of innocent babies, very young children, whether it was a purposeful act by some very evil person, or an accident, and you just wonder, where is God when all of this is happening? Has He abandoned us, or have we abandoned him?"

"Those are some of the most important questions of our time," I responded.

"They are, and I certainly don't have any answers. I just keep praying every day, but more and more it seems that prayers aren't enough anymore. Like that saying, what was it, 'It rains on the good and the evil alike,' or something like that?"

"Sounds about right," I said.

"We can ask why bad things happen to good people. But not even that, we can also ask why bad things happen to completely innocent people, to children and babies? Those were the things that were tough to get over during my career, when kids died. And I've got a story I could tell you along those lines, not about something that happened in the line of duty, but something that happened in my personal life that just made me mad as hell at God."

"Yeah, if you're comfortable sharing it, by all means," I said.

"Okay. Well, so one of my fellow officer's daughters was born around the same time as one of my teenagers, one who's still at home, and she had a debilitating disease that affects a lot of children, I won't say what it was, out of respect for their privacy. We were really close with the family. Now my son, he has genetic disorders which have caused him to be visually impaired, and so he goes to the school for the blind, and we used to call her Ian's little girlfriend because they were almost the same age. But one day the family called us, and we found out that she was dying, and it was going to be the end of the road very soon. So we all went to Children's to say our goodbyes, because they were going to turn the machines off and let her die in comfort so she wouldn't have to suffer anymore. And it was heart-wrenching, just to see this innocent little life, who was sick and had only known suffering in her young life. You have to ask why. I mean, you can think about the big picture, you know, she was brought here for a reason, it could have brought their marriage closer together, could have done a lot of things, but I couldn't understand the reason for God taking her, and it made me mad. And I lost a little faith, you know? I'm slowly regaining it since I've retired but you know, I still don't understand how all these people out here, ones that I don't know personally, you see all this suffering, and you say, if there is a God, why is He letting all this happen? So I can almost see other people's despair and why they're losing faith too, it used to be that you could turn to the church, but now there's theft and stuff, people stealing from the churches. They're breaking into the safes, they're going into the Catholic churches up to the altars and stealing candlesticks and communion cups and stuff, and they're stealing the boxes that are by the candles that people put money into when they say a prayer, they're stealing everything. And so the churches have locked their doors now, they're not open like they used to be. Used to be that you could walk into a church and say, 'help me.' Now if someone does that they have to call a police officer and have them guard the priest at three in the morning.

It's just a sad state of affairs that we're in at this point. Makes you wonder."

His voice trailed off.

Raised Catholic myself, it did make me wonder. I transported myself back to my hometown church and imagined the doors being locked up every night. What was more distressing about his monologue, though, was how true it all sounded. The church is not the sacred place it once was, and although there is always great work done by charities in service to the poor and marginalized in society, these campaigns do not seem to be making a substantial impact on the quality of life of the least among us. On a more positive note, it does still seem to be true that on an individual and familial level, the church has continued to work miracles. However, in the face of the poverty and destitution Charles witnessed on his daily patrols, it is clear that their efforts alone do not constitute a solution. It seems that we all need to step up and make an effort to help our fellow man.

Chapter Nine

"The dark side of duty"

      In one of our final interviews, which happened in late April of 2018, the time had come for what I anticipated would be one of the most difficult discussions for Charles, due to the subject matter. As if some of our previous conversations hadn't included enough disturbing characters and narratives, we were about to engage with all of the demons Charles had been doing battle with in his mind for his entire life. He already saw a psychologist and a rehab specialist once a week, addressing his mental and physical scars, respectively, and now he had to sit down with me, and go over the worst of the worst of them. To say I was unprepared for this day was an understatement, and I could not even begin to imagine how Charles was feeling.

      "So this is it. The dark side of duty," I said. "I know this is going to be really personal, and I don't want you to share anything you aren't comfortable with putting out there. So just, let it flow from you naturally, don't force anything, just talk about it, and we'll sort it all out later," I advised him.

      I could tell that he was nervous, but in a positive way, if that was possible.

      "I'm ready, believe me, I want to get this out there," he said. "I want people to know how this really affects you as an officer. It's not like we're law enforcement robots out there with no emotions. We're human beings."

      "Of course."

Charles took a deep breath.

"So, what do I mean by the dark side of duty? Well, what people need to understand is that police officers are there for the worst parts of your life, for the worst things that happen to you. They come to your door over domestic issues, over arguments, or they come when you're ending your relationship and a standby is needed so nobody gets hurt or gets falsely accused of anything. They come for when a baby dies of SIDS, for when someone commits suicide, or when your grandparent passes away. Sadness, tragedy, and death is a part of our daily job. Sometimes we would see more death in one week than most people see in a lifetime. And I hate to say it, but at some point, it just becomes normal, especially when it was an adult. When it was a young child victim, it really bothered you, the suicide of a young person, it bothered you. When it was an elderly gentleman or woman who passed away naturally, you got used to that, those weren't so bad. But it was overdoses, car accidents with adults, violent domestic altercations, some of that shit just became normal, and that's kind of fucked up, right? But death was a part of life on this job, somebody has to notify the family, somebody has to make sure there is no foul play involved, and our fine men and women in the police are the people who get to do that, so the members of the public don't have to. We are there for the darkest moments in people's lives. We are there for every aspect of the entire process of dealing with death in society."

"Yeah, I never thought about it like that before," I responded. "It's almost like going to a thousand funerals."

"More than that," Charles said.

"Well, how do you even act in those situations, then? When you're with family members and their son or daughter or father or mother has died, and you've seen death a thousand times yourself. And in your case, you've almost shut yourself off to it, to being emotionally affected by it."

"The way to do it is just to be respectful, to be solemn, you know. If you have an officer who is quiet and reserved at the scene of a death or a suicide, it's not because they don't care, it's because they're doing their job, they're trying to be respectful and moral. It's part of our job to console the families and help them through it, but it's not an easy task. The suffering is so great."

"You'd think you guys would get some kind of bonus or hazard pay for doing that job, that's almost a whole other profession, being a community psychologist too," I said.

Charles nodded.

"That's right, it's one of the many hats that officers wear."

"How do you deal with the exposure to that much tragedy?" I asked.

"It's difficult to deal with alone. You see officers trying to kill the memories with alcohol, but alcohol is a depressant, it won't make the bad memories go away, alcohol makes it worse, and that's why cops lead all professions in divorce, suicide, and alcoholism. It's a sacrifice that you make. People think that a sacrifice for a cop is giving your life, the greatest sacrifice, but every day of your life is a sacrifice in some respects, because you're taking these things which normal people don't have to be burdened with, all of the tragedies and deaths and pain and tears, and you're folding all of that into your own mind and your own heart as you experience the grief with them, because you can't avoid it. You respond to a call, whatever it is, and whatever is happening, you can't just leave or run away, you have to stay, you have to."

"So then, what about the physical part of the job?" I asked. "Being an officer means you have to be able to hold your ground in altercations, chase people down, restrain people, and that has taken a toll on your body over the years, I'm sure."

"More than a toll, it's been brutal."

I nodded. It was time to discuss the events which caused him to be in the state of constant pain I saw before me. The physical part of it, at any rate.

"Do you want to talk about the surgeries now?" I asked. "Or at least, you know, the reasons why you had to have them?"

"Yeah, I can tell you about all that," he paused. "So, it had been a pretty long career at that point when my first major health crisis occurred, in the year 2013, getting close to twenty years in as a police officer in our city. After many years in the military, riding around in those rattle-trap tanks, and all those years as an officer getting in scuffles and fights and falling off of things, getting in car wrecks and foot pursuits and shootings, it all caught up to me over the course of one day. Just a regular day, I was getting in my cruiser, and it was parked tightly next to another cruiser, and so I had to kind of slide my way in through the narrow gap of the door, and when I twisted my body sideways to slide in, I felt a pop in my neck, and then a burning under my skin in my neck and shoulders. It was ungodly, excruciating pain. So I went in and talked to my supervisor, told him what was going on, and went down to the local pharmacy and got some of those hot and ice patches, you know, to see if it was maybe something minor I could get through, I had been hurt so many times working that it was just like, 'shake it off and go,' right? So I used all the patches I bought and finished off my shift, but later that night, the burning came back with such intensity, just unimaginable pain, that I hit the ground, and collapsed on the floor of my kitchen. So, I pretty much forced myself to get up and get into my car and drive to the hospital, they did x-rays and gave me shots in the area, to get the burning to stop so I could at least function. I probably got home from the hospital around two in the morning, and thank God I was off the next day. Was in a lot of pain still, and my mobility and range of motion in my neck and my arms was just not feeling at all normal. But then the following evening, once again, I hit the kitchen floor in horrible pain, and this time I couldn't even drive, so my wife had to take me. Went back in for more x-rays and cat scans and MRI's and everything else, and next thing I know I was referred to a surgeon."

"That was when you knew it was serious," I commented.

"Yeah, it wasn't a very good feeling. I was hopeful that it wouldn't be anything bad, but unfortunately it was. I went to the surgeon and he explained that I had a bad case of degenerative disc disease, and that the C4-C5 and the C5-C6 had collapsed on my spinal cord, causing scarring and nerve damage, and so now, as a result of that, the nerves that run through my left arm on the inside are totally numb now, but that was the least of my worries at the time. So, we had the first surgery, and they put in plates and screws in the C4-C5 and C5-C6, and they did a partial fusion, and so I was off for four months, and then I went back to work after that period of time, thinking I was still me, but now I was part Terminator, you know?"

"Had to have a positive attitude about it," I said.

"Had to, for sure. So I worked from then until 2015, so it was roughly a year and a half, eighteen months, and then, the C2-C3, C3-C4, C6-C7 and C7-T1, all of those discs collapsed on me. I thought the pain was bad before, but I'll tell you what, the pain I had this time around, I wouldn't even wish on my worst enemy. So, I went in for a second surgery, they tore everything off from the first one, and they went in and put in five more plates, twenty screws, and they totally fused my neck from the base of my head down to my shoulders. Told me I had a forty percent chance of coming out of that surgery paralyzed, but I beat those odds. Still, it was hell on my body of course, I was ventilated and kept in the Intensive Care Unit for thirty-seven hours, and every time I woke up and started fighting and trying to pull the tubes out they would have to get a bunch of nurses to hold me down so they could put more drugs in me. I woke up thinking that it was the Friday night on the day of the surgery, but it was actually Sunday."

"That's crazy. I mean your body had to take it's time to recover, there's no rushing that, especially after surgery in such a delicate area," I said.

"It wasn't fun, that's for sure. So that Sunday, I got out of the hospital, went home, and I was off work for five months, I think. And when I decided I was ready to go back to work, I found out the hard way, just being out there on the streets again, that I just wasn't me anymore. I wasn't as strong as I used to be, I wasn't as agile and quick on my feet, and I would have ended up as a risk to myself and others being physically compromised and unable to perform my duties up to the standards of my former abilities. One more physical encounter with a suspect, one more scuffle and I would probably would have been done for, might have injured myself for good and ended up in a wheelchair. But I pushed myself for as long as I could, for about six months. And then, in July of 2016, my father passed away from cancer. He had wanted me to retire so badly, and I had started the process before he had died, and it was just tough to have both of those things happening at the same time."

"Yeah definitely, I'm sure it was. Can you tell me about what happened with your dad, then?"

"Sure," Charles said. He removed his glasses and put them back on, for no discernible reason, but probably just to steel himself for the next few minutes. I knew that this part especially was going to be extremely difficult for him, seeing as we were only a couple of years removed from the event.

"Actually, it was June of 2016 originally when we got the call that he had cancer. Stage three, lung cancer, and the doctors said they would try the best they could, but the cancer was obviously at an advanced stage, so there weren't a wide range of options for him. So, when we told him the news, he decided he wanted to get out of town, he wanted to get away for a bit, and so we said 'okay, let's go,' and as a family we pooled our vacation money and rented a beach house on the Outer Banks in North Carolina for a week. Brought down as much family as we could get together, had a wonderful week on this beach house overlooking the ocean. Dad and I would sneak out every morning and fish at the pier nearby, we were catching small sharks and Spanish mackerels, and that was probably the best time of my life that I got to talk to him, you know, we would just spend hours fishing and talking, it was the best bonding time I ever had with him."

His voice trailed off, and he was silent for a few seconds.

"We got back in the beginning of July, we got back from the vacation, and I returned home, and the doctors kept me updated, they said they would have him on radiation treatments, and they were saying that there was a shot that the radiation might knock this tumor out. But what happened was, he was on warfarin, which he had to take after he had a heart attack, and when they hit him with the first dose of radiation, the tumor started to bleed, and when I got word of that, I went down to Nashville, going a hundred miles an hour, turned a five-hour drive into a four-hour drive. Went into the hospital room he was at, my mom and my brother were there, and the doctors told us that there was basically nothing they could do, if they tried surgery he would bleed even more and likely die on the operating table, and my dad looked at me, and asked me 'Am I dying?" and I said "Yes sir." And he said, "Okay." He wanted some food, he wanted some mashed potatoes and gravy and some ice cream, and the nurse actually told him he couldn't have it, but I talked to the doctor and was able to persuade them to get him some, and so they did, and he had a bite of each, a spoonful of mashed potatoes and a spoonful of ice cream, and that was the last thing he ate for seven days. We were at his bedside the whole time. Most of the time he was either sleeping or just barely conscious and staring off into space, not saying much. We kept telling him it was okay to go, that he shouldn't be afraid, and he wasn't, but we were, so we had to keep telling him that for our sakes, you know? We signed him up for hospice so we could at least try and get him home, they had a five day hospice period at the hospital before we could get the equipment sent to the house. We went and bought his urn as well, because he wanted to be cremated, and so we got a big, beautiful urn with red, white and blue mosaic tile. The last thing he said to me was "Take care of your mom, and keep the family together." On the last day of his life, we had decided to go back home for a few hours, Mom hadn't slept in days, she was completely worn out, and so I told her 'just sleep, I got my phone on me, don't worry.' And I sat in my dad's rocking chair by the fireplace, and it hadn't been but five minutes that I sat down that the phone rang, and they said, 'Charles, your dad just took his last breath.'"

Charles took off his glasses again, wiping away a couple tears from his eyes, and bowed his head, as if he was ashamed and didn't want me to see. It was the only time he had shown visible emotion during any of our interviews, but I wasn't surprised that this was the breaking point for the walls he had built up. He used to tell me straightforwardly that he was still in denial that his father was dead, and that was to say nothing about the mental state of his mother. As always, I was conflicted about the decision to ask him to recall these memories, and wondered whether he would be able to continue with the interview.

He carried on.

"My mom had heard me talking on the phone with the doctors, and she came out in her nightgown, and was yelling, "What, what?" And I told her, and she collapsed, and I was yelling down the hall for my brother and my cousins who were there with us. We got her together as best we could, got her in the car and all went to the hospital. We went into the room, and I prayed over him, and we let mom say her goodbyes, and my brother and I said ours, and the rest of the family said theirs. Had my cousins take my mom out of the hospital and back home when it was all said and done, because I didn't want her to see a sight that I had seen a hundred thousand times, which was my dad being put in a bag and taken to the morgue, but this time it was my dad, not a crime victim. Had to sign over the body, and I placed the urn gently on top of dad's stomach, and then I worked my way out to the elevator and out of the hospital. And like I said, we had him cremated, so later on we went and picked up his urn, and put a cross on top of the urn, and I put his dog tags and his Navy ring on top of it as well, and picked up his flag from the VA."

"Where did you guys put him, in a mausoleum, or did you bury the urn?"

"No, we didn't bury him, he's at home with mom now. And we were down there for another two weeks to help her recover, she didn't know how to live after being with someone for over fifty years. After she was mentally and physically ready, we came back up here to Cincinnati for the memorial service, did that at my brother's church, and then afterwards we went to a restaurant, but I wasn't feeling good at all, felt like I was about to collapse, and so I left and got my son to take me home. And then I had to go back to work."

"I don't even know how you did it, Charles." I shook my head.

"I don't know either. My body wasn't working, my brain wasn't working, dad's gone, but I just have to put all that aside, bury it deep inside me so I can do the job I'm supposed to do as a police officer, to be there for everybody else's traumas and traumatic events, craziness going on in their world. Then the retirement came through, finally. The retirement that my dad had begged me to do but he never got to see. And I miss Sir. He's not here anymore for me to ask him questions when I need advice, he's not there for my brother or for my mom. He was the rock of our family, and now he's gone. And I didn't know what to do with myself."

Several more moments of silence followed.

"Well, it must have made you feel good then, earning the retirement must have taken a ton of weight off you," I suggested.

Charles shrugged.

"Well, see, let me tell you something about retirement. At least for me, and other officers will know what I'm talking about if they've been through some of the things that I've been through, you might be trying to forget all the messed-up shit you've seen, you may be trying to move on with a new chapter in your life, you might be trying to move into your golden years. But the problem is that, the demons still find you. They still come and haunt you in the night, while you sleep. I have constant nightmares about everything horrific that I saw during my career, and they never go away no matter how much I wish and pray that they would. I wake up suffocating, and I can feel, literally feel the pain of pieces of burning plaster falling on my head and skin, and I'm sucking air and gasping for breath like I'm still in the fire. A lot of the ones that haunt me, like the blue baby, the woman keeps coming at me with her dead baby, and no matter where I turn, she's there with the dead baby coming at me again, carrying the little boy like he was a log, and just rolled him right on the grass to me. The words echoing, 'Save my baby, Bell.' She used my name, and those words and that baby will never stop coming to me at night. The guy who shot himself in the heart, there was a girl who slit her wrists in the bathtub, and you couldn't even tell that she was in water, there was so much blood. I see these people in my dreams, and their eyes open, and when they open, I think they're going to tell me why they did what they did, but then I wake up in a cold sweat before they say anything. It's terrible, and I can never escape them, no matter what I do. You can't run from it, you can't hide from it, retirement is not running from the demons, it's the opposite. It's meeting them face to face. The demons know who you are, where you are, and they have no mercy, they never stop coming. I've had medicine prescribed by my psychiatrist to try and stop them, but the medication had no effect. And, I get nightmares about everything else too, not just the horrific stuff. My brain goes over and over about decisions I should or should not have made, about the 'what ifs' and the questions of 'why' and 'how' and 'what the fuck.' I see my fellow officer's casket go down into the ground like I did with countless other of my friends, a guy I went to high school with, had a lot of great memories with, laughing and joking and looking forward to whatever life would have in store for us, and then both of us choosing to become police officers, and now, he's dead in a box, killed in the line of duty. It's a career that some people think is a walk in the park, and television shows try to sensationalize it, glorify it, make it look exciting and sexy. But that's not what it's like at all. It's not fabulous, it's not awesome. What's so awesome about walking into a house and having to comfort family members when their son has killed themselves, or someone with Hepatitis telling you that they have it after they've spit in your face or coughed blood all over you? You know, it's wonderful, it's great, such a glorious career! But in the end, truly, I can say, I don't regret any of that, because I went into the job thinking I could help people, and I think I did. I believe I was successful in the goal I set for myself, the goal to make a difference in as many people's lives as I could. So no, I don't regret any of it. But, I do suffer. People see a cop out on the street, people who hate cops, or even people who don't, and they see a cop, and they probably don't know what we go through. They see a cop who's just a regular guy or a regular gal, and we're just out there doing a job, and we're doing it for you, we do this to help people, to protect and serve. Why hate us? Because we gave you a parking ticket? The guy who wrote you that parking ticket, you don't know that he went home later that night, drank a bunch of beer and stuck a gun in his mouth, but then decided not to do it, and that's what happens. So maybe think about that before you look at a cop in disgust when they're out on patrol. We're doing the best we can, and that's all I have to say about that."

Chapter Ten

"Retirement"

"So I wanted to talk some more about your retirement years, if you don't mind?"

Charles and I were about to meet for one last time, after which we decided that we had enough stories recorded to move forward with the book. He had walked through my door on that final interview day with an uncommon buoyancy about him, something that I was happy to see, given that I could never quite predict what state of mind he would bring to my apartment. There were a few more questions I wanted to ask him during that last session, along with engaging in some last-minute fact-checking, and confirmation or denial of specific details about one story or another. However, if I'm being truly honest, I set up our last meeting because I wanted to hear something positive out of him about the end of his career and the weeks and months after he left the police force. Really, just anything remotely sanguine I could get out of him, I would have considered it a victory.

Charles looked out the window before turning his attention back to me.

"Sure, what do you need to know?" he asked.

"Well, I guess, just how you were feeling on the day it happened, on your last day of work perhaps, or wherever you want to start. What were the main thoughts going through your mind at the time, and what were you looking forward to in the future?"

He adjusted his glasses, and then put his hand over his fist and his elbows on the table in a reflective pose.

"Well, so, here's the thing. When I stepped out of our precinct headquarters for the last time, I was basically stepping out into a whole new world. In a lot of ways, I was just beginning a process of losing my identity, because, of course, the military service aside, I had always done this, I had always been a police officer, and now I was a civilian. It was almost as if I suddenly had no idea who I was. I had to find myself again, or create a new me, somehow."

"It was probably very similar to when military servicemen and women come back to civilian life from war," I pointed out.

"Certainly," Charles said. "When a service member leaves a war zone and comes back into the fold of society, it can be incredibly difficult to adjust. For me, it's still difficult to ignore my old instincts as a police officer when I'm just going about my daily life. I'll give you an example here actually. Well, I guess this doesn't have to do with my retirement, but it's more about being off duty."

"That's fine," I said, "I'm sure the same concepts apply."

Charles nodded.

"So, the issue with being a cop is that you're never off duty. You see things happening when you're going about your day, and even if you don't have your uniform on, you can still have a positive impact on the situation. One day, my wife and I were walking into the entrance of a grocery store, and a manager runs by us, almost knocking into my cart, as he is running over to the exit to the store to approach a pair of male shoplifters. I look over and I see a female loss prevention officer in a physical struggle with the two shoplifters, and my wife looks up at me and says,

'Charles, they need help.' And so I went over and announced myself as a police officer, and the manager and loss prevention officer were asserting that the two males had tucked items into their clothing, and so I stepped in and asked the shoplifters if they had indeed stolen anything, which they denied. What I ended up having to do was physically restrain them myself without the use of handcuffs so they could be searched, because a witness had reported their behavior to the management, and so that provided the loss prevention officer with reason enough to initiate a search of their persons. So I began to control one of the suspects using a joint control technique I had developed to limit the arm movement capabilities of individuals, which served the dual purpose of making it very difficult to escape my grasp. And they were searched and were found to have items on them which they had not paid for, and so they got to take a ride in a police car. So, you know, that's just one example, like I said, it's not from after I retired, but it's relevant."

"Definitely," I said. "Well, and I mean, I'm sure you were trying to find a new purpose for yourself as well, to replace the sense of purpose you had as an officer?"

"Trying to find my purpose was another thing, too, for sure. Giving up the badge was equivalent to me giving up my purpose in life, and that was a hard and bitter truth. I used to be helping people and had the authority to step in and save the day in a crisis, but when I retired, it just seemed like I was almost helpless, I would see the issues play out on the streets, see the problems I was addressing every day as a cop, and now not being able to do anything about what I was seeing, that was frustrating. I was just a hot mess when I retired. I was running down to Tennessee every weekend to see my mom, because she wasn't over my dad's death by any means, she didn't know how to function after being with somebody for fifty-four years. So I was running down there, and still had a family to raise, had some marital difficulties, and life was just wearing me down."

Unfortunately, no positivity in sight.

"I guess, maybe, your purpose now is to finish raising your kids?" I ventured.

Charles laughed.

"Well that's one way to look at it. My kids are everything to me now."

I nodded.

This junction in the conversation made me think about the stage of life Charles was currently going through, a stage which every parent reaches at some point in their life, one which my own parents were near to reaching themselves. Of course, everyone struggles with finding their purpose, no matter what age they are or what station in society they find themselves. Being able to realize your potential as a human being, what some might call self-actualization, is a common indicator of mental and physical good health. For some fathers and mothers, the job of raising their kids into successful adults might be an integral part of their process of self-actualization. Add to that a fulfilling career, maybe a few grandkids later on, and generally, that seems to do the trick. For others, in the life after kids, there might not be enough time in the universe to discover the entirety of the meaning of their existence, and for still more unfortunate souls, their lives have been defined to such an overwhelming degree by bad luck or ill health or failure, that they give up their search for purpose, and balance on the precipice of the abyss until death. I had the feeling that Charles was in an ill-defined grey area on this spectrum of fulfillment. By all his accounts, Charles seemed to be satisfied with his career in the military, with his career as an officer, and with being a father. All of his kids and grandkids were enough to ensure that his lifetime of wisdom and experiences would not be forgotten by future generations. However, Charles had suffered a lot in his life, and his mind and body were in constant pain. He would often refer to his life before the surgeries as 'the time before the pain,' which is really an incredible statement. Furthermore, I was beginning to see that this chronic condition might have been enough to cancel out any feelings of achievement or happiness resulting from his life in the time before the pain. And that, I think, is one of the real tragedies of Charles' life.

After having all of those thoughts running through my head, I again tried to steer the conversation toward hopefully more cheerful topics.

"Well, my friend, I was hoping to hear about some positive things that came about after your retirement," I said. "I know it was a trying time for you, but surely there was, you know, some joy in there somewhere?"

Charles smiled.

"I guess there were some good things. It was very freeing to retire, I will say that, despite everything that was going on. I knew I might eventually have to go back to work at some point to make some extra money, but I had a lot of hope for the future. I thought I was going to be fishing all the time, relaxing, taking care of the kids, barbequing on the weekends, all that stuff. Actually, now that I mention fishing, I guess I do have a good retirement story for you. My teenagers still laugh at this one, it's pretty great."

"Go right ahead."

He cleared his throat.

"So, it was, I think it was the first or second week out of my retirement, and I didn't really know what I wanted to do with all my newfound free time, other than like I said, to go fishing all the time, which I was really excited about. So one day I went out to a local river, and it was an absolutely beautiful morning, and I'm on top of the world, just feeling really good about life. All my gear was in good shape, I was in the water, looking at the natural splendor, there was a blue heron across from me on the other side, and I guess there were also a couple eagles nesting in the area, which would have been a great sight to see. And what that also means of course, with all of those predatory birds in one location, that means there's definitely fish in the water."

"So you had a good day of fishing then?" I asked.

"Well, I would have, if not for an unfortunate accident that befell me. So, here's what happens. I'm walking upstream toward this rocky island that's in the middle of the river, where it splits the current in two, because I wanted to set up on it and fish from there. I had been walking in the river but near to the bank, and I wanted to get to the island, and so I decided, 'well, there are a lot of rocks and boulders but it's only a foot and a half, two feet deep, so it can't be too dangerous.' Well, that didn't end up going so well for Old Charles."

I cracked a smile and a bit of a laugh.

"The current was fast, and it was only after a few steps going across that I slipped on a rock. The water wasn't clear, it wasn't murky, but there wasn't the best visibility to see the bottom. I violated the number one rule, which is to not step through water if you can't see the bottom, so I guess I got what was coming to me. Anyway, so I slipped on the rock, and my boots went out from under me, and all of the sudden I'm horizontal. My waders are filling up fast with water, and the current is washing me down, my head is going under the water and back up again as I'm clawing at the rocks and trying to half-push, half-swim my way toward the shore. Finally, I get to a point where I can get up and get out of the water, and all the water is gushing out of my waders, I'm about a hundred feet down from the island, and I pull out my cigarettes, they're soaked. And I just sit down and think for a second, because it's kind of funny, you know? After all the shit I went through in my career, almost getting shot, getting burned, getting knifed, getting hit by cars, and it's actually two feet of water and a fast current while I'm fishing that ends up killing me! Nothing else killed me, but retirement did! Anyway, I thought it was funny."

"Yeah, that was a good one. Fishing will always be there for us, right?" I've been an outdoorsman for my whole life, and so I could relate to the contentment he felt with the water below him, foliage around him, and the blue sky above him. Well at least, before his foothold was betrayed by a mossy boulder.

"Always," Charles said. "Let's me and you take a trip this summer, you want to? I can show you all the spots I used to go to near my mother's house down in Tennessee. There are some beautiful rivers and streams down there, it's absolutely gorgeous."

"Sounds like a plan, my friend," I said. "Sounds like a plan to me."

The End

Made in the USA
Middletown, DE
15 November 2018